Success is Just the Beginning

6 Timeless Lessons to Achieve More in Business, Love, and Legacy

Stephanie P. Kemp

Saved By Story

Published by
Saved By Story Publishing, LLC
Prescott, AZ

www.SavedByStory.house

Cover by Alyssa Noelle Coelho
Interior Design by Dawn Teagarden

Disclaimer: The Publisher and the Author does not guarantee that anyone following the techniques, suggestions, tips, ideas or strategies will become successful. The advice and strategies contained herein may not be suitable for every situation. The Publisher and Author shall have neither liability nor responsibility to anyone with respect to any loss or damage caused, or alleged to be caused, directly or indirectly by the information in this book. Written permission has been obtained to share the identity of each real individual named in this book.

Any citations or a potential source of information from other organizations or websites given herein does not mean that the Author or Publisher endorses the information/content the website or organization provides or recommendations it may make. It is the readers' responsibility to do their own due diligence when researching information. Also, websites listed or referenced herein may have changed or disappeared from the time that this work was created and the time that it is read.

Library of Congress Control Number: 2023909390
Hardback ISBN: 978-1-961336-01-8
Paperback ISBN: 978-1-961336-00-1
eBook ISBN: 978-1-961336-02-5

Printed in the United States of America

www.SavedByStory.house

To the people who lift me out of holes:
My husband, Michael Wiseman,
my children, Rhett and Cierra Wiseman,
and my brother, Christian Kemp.

Lucky me.

A Special Invitation from Stephanie

If you are serious about shattering the status quo and sustaining your success…

Visit www.StephaniePKemp.com to:

- download questions designed to help you integrate the six timeless lessons in this book into your business and life
- watch our world-class dancers from NEDA Nation and witness the impact of these lessons on young people with big dreams
- learn more about NEDA Nation and the opportunity to franchise and grow your own sustained success with us
- check out my other wealth-oiled machines that are breaking the status quo and sustaining success

CONTENTS

Prologue
"I've Seen the Way Out" 7

Introduction
It's Time to Build Your Wealth-Oiled Machine 9

Chapter 1
Will and Work Ethic 15

Chapter 2
Expectations and Equity 33

Chapter 3
Aim and Accountability 51

Chapter 4
Love and Loyalty 67

Chapter 5
Time and Trouble 83

Chapter 6
Habits and Humans 103

Conclusion
Leave a Wealth-Oiled Dent in the Mattress 119

About the Author 123

A Special Invitation from Stephanie 124

Acknowledgments 125

When I stand before God at the end of my life, I would hope that I would not have a single bit of talent left, and could say, "I used everything you gave me."

Erma Bombeck

PROLOGUE

"I'VE SEEN THE WAY OUT"

A young, driven entrepreneur was charging down the sidewalk, coffee in one hand, phone in the other, and a heavy purse slung over her shoulder. She had her daily to-do lists and, as usual, was trying to accomplish everything in record time. She was so focused on her next destination, she missed the orange cones and dropped straight down into a hole that had been masked on the sidewalk. Shocked and stunned, she picked herself up and wiped the coffee off her face. Immediately, she realized she'd lost her phone in the fall, so she tried climbing her way up out of the hole. But she couldn't.

As the minutes turned into hours and she still couldn't see her way out, she became desperate. She clawed and scraped at the sides of the hole. She tried to lift herself out again. But the more she tried, the deeper she sank into the pit.

As the day turned into night, she became frightened and began frantically yelling out for help. "Is anyone up there? I have fallen into this deep hole and I can't get out."

She yelled for hours. Finally, her doctor appeared.

She cried, "Doctor! I've fallen into this deep hole and I can't get out!"

The doctor quickly wrote her a prescription, threw it down into the hole, and then walked away.

Feeling even more defeated and overwhelmed, she cried out even louder. "Can someone please help me? I'm trapped in this hole and I can't find my way out!"

Suddenly, her priest was there.

"Father, can you help me? I've fallen into this deep hole and I can't find my way out."

The priest bowed his head and said, "I will pray for you, my child." Then he was gone.

Now convinced that her family would never get her back in one piece, she became frantic. Even though she was tired, hungry, and thirsty, she attempted to pull herself out again and again but to no avail. So she screamed for help yet again. "Is there anyone up there? I've fallen into this deep hole and I can't find my way out."

Suddenly, an older woman peered in.

"Do you think you could help me? I've fallen so deep, I can't seem to find my way out," the younger woman cried.

Without hesitation, the older woman jumped into the hole. The younger woman was shocked and dismayed. "Now we're both stuck in this hole!"

The older woman replied, "Yes, but I have been here before, and I've seen the way out."

INTRODUCTION

It's Time to Build Your Wealth-Oiled Machine

Women have come a long way in entrepreneurship since I opened my first business more than thirty years ago. We've shattered many stereotypes and proven our worth as successful business leaders. Even so, being an entrepreneur is not for the faint of heart. Building a solid business—a business that can sustain success—remains an uphill battle. A battle that is sometimes riddled with pain and drama. A battle that is sometimes lost. But there is good news: *success leaves clues.*

If you're anything like me, you are driven by the desire to build a successful business that not only provides financial independence but also allows you to pursue your passions, create a positive impact in your community, enjoy the freedom to honor your family, your schedule, and your bank account, and most importantly, provides you the opportunity to align your personal and professional objectives.

You're Not Selfish

I am here to tell you that wanting to live a balanced life is not a selfish desire. A life showered with personal and professional achievements is not only possible, it's imperative. Whether you're just starting out or a seasoned business owner, I believe your success is inextricably linked to your health and happiness. So isn't it time to redefine your idea of success?

Your *success* in business, love, and legacy.

I may not know you personally, but I know you because I was you.

I know your desire for abundance, love, and creativity. I taste your hunger for excellence. I smell your fear of disappointment. And I see the opportunities that are within your grasp if only you have the courage to *stretch* for them.

I never thought I would write a book. I don't have an MBA, and I'm not a psychologist, but I am a serial entrepreneur with the heart of a teacher. Although I love to get inspiration and motivation from the well-known billionaires, I often find myself yearning to hear more success stories of the people who fell under the radar. People who aimed high and persevered over time. People in the trenches with real-time experiences. People who found success in business and then sustained it. People who realized *success is just the beginning*—that getting to the top is easy, but surviving on top is the real challenge.

I've always been a success seeker, inspired by the people who made it look easy and measured their success not only in monetary value but in the value of relationships—relationships that were earned and relationships that endured. So I'm sharing my journey in hopes that my story may help other entrepreneurs find the courage to live the life of their dreams on their terms.

First and foremost, I consider myself an educator. I was called to this earth to stand with children and, more recently, with entrepreneurs because I believe all people have the capacity for greatness when taught empowering lessons and given opportunities to rise. Sometimes we fall and sometimes we lose. And yet we can be taught to persevere until we achieve our dreams.

While I share stories from my early days in my first business in the dance studio industry, the lessons in this book are applicable to any business. The parallels, strategies, and techniques I share have catapulted my success from start-up to scale-up, service to product, one team member to one hundred.

A Successful Life Is a Life Rich in Relationships

Building a successful business is no different than building a successful relationship. A relationship that sustains. A relationship that grows. A relationship that weathers the test of time.

If you want hypergrowth, then you have to be willing to be a hyperleader. Someone who inspires those around them to greatness. Someone who doesn't just settle for what is expected. Someone who expects more.

Over time, I realized my success was contingent on developing what I call a "wealth-oiled machine" that would sustain the successes in my personal and professional life. I'm not talking about a financial statement or a balance sheet. I'm talking about principles that challenged me to reach higher, be better, and do better for the people I was called to serve. These lessons have helped me create an impact and live a life of love, prosperity, and legacy.

Although I don't pretend to have all the answers, I will share these timeless lessons I have tested over several decades in business—lessons that have helped me build wealth in every area of my life.

Will Power and **W**ork Ethic

Expectations and **E**quity

Aim and **A**ccountability

Love and **L**oyalty

Time and **T**rouble

Habits and **H**umans

We all have the power to create something extraordinary. In this book, I share not only my story but also my journey, proving you don't have to be a genius, a millionaire, or a mathematician to win in business. If it's a wealth-oiled machine you seek, these six timeless lessons are easy to access, easy to follow, and easy to repeat.

I built my own wealth-oiled machine by learning from others' failures and by avoiding unnecessary drama and pain. By making mistakes and then learning from them so I didn't repeat them. My wealth-oiled machine is made of a series of gears that grind and grind and yet continue to carry my weight. When the gears get stuck and the motor stalls, I am quick to oil and quick to recharge because I know little and big humans are relying on me to keep the gears in motion.

I've spent my entire life as a mentor, teacher, and coach, and I've built successful businesses by helping others realize their full potential. But there is one thing you should know about me before we get started: *I don't sugarcoat the truth.* If you have picked up this book looking for the easy solutions, you've come to the wrong place. This book is for people who are eager to push boundaries, even if that means stretching into uncomfortable positions.

I always play to win, which means I never play "not to lose." I won't play it safe or soft here because I believe, as entrepreneurs, we have a responsibility to do better and be better for the people we are called upon to serve.

This is the straight-talking advice I wish I'd had as a young entrepreneur. A young entrepreneur who was wildly ambitious. A young entrepreneur who was hungry for opportunity. A young entrepreneur who was driven to make a difference.

I suspect readers will pick up this book at varying stages of their journey, so let me save you the anticipation—I can't protect you from the holes or save you from the slips and the falls. And the simple truth is, I wouldn't want to. The entrepreneurial journey isn't easy, but I believe it is through the challenges and setbacks that I became stronger, braver, and more resilient. I fell. I slipped. And I got stuck, but I always got back up. With a strong support system of like-minded individuals who have seen the way out once or twice before, I learned to pull myself out of life's holes.

You may look at my story and call it luck. I choose to call it work. *Working with what I have.*

Even when it's hard and things appear to be slipping, I choose to only focus on the blessings and lessons that have helped me prevail. I don't see the glass as half-empty or half-full. I merely see a simple glass—a glass with room to add more.

You may be tempted to compare your circumstances to mine and think, "But I don't have… " Regardless of where you're starting, I believe you can use the principles and strategies in this book to work with what you have and develop a wealth mindset. This mindset will allow you to see more opportunities than you do now.

When you hear yourself say, "But I don't have…," I implore you to shift your focus to what you *do* have to work with right now. It may take some creativity to find and utilize the resources you do have, and it may take you longer than it took me or others to build a wealth-oiled machine, but I believe we all have what it takes to generate more success for our business and our life.

Although I share my own experiences and strategies, the point is not for you to follow my path exactly. Instead, I encourage you to take the principles and solutions presented through my stories and apply them to your own life, on your own timetable, on your own terms, supported by people who will pull you up when the holes are deep.

From my humble beginnings to a life filled with opportunity, I will show you firsthand that it's not where you've been that matters—it's where you are going. Where you're focused. Where you're committed. From this day forward, you get to choose. Choose to settle, or choose more.

So here is your invitation. Your invitation to live a life rich in passion and purpose. An invitation to take my hand and let me help you build your own wealth-oiled machine.

I'm excited for your journey and honored for the opportunity to support you. Let the wealth-building begin!

CHAPTER 1

WILL AND WORK ETHIC

The Show Must Go On

It was a beautiful day in June 1991. I'd been waiting for this day for what seemed like my whole life. It was a celebration day, a day of uncontrollable excitement mixed with anxiety. Ten months before, I'd opened my first business—a dance studio—and today was showtime. It was the big show day. But not just any show day; it was the very first show day. This was the day I got to prove to the entire community why picking me, why taking the "leap" with me, why entrusting me with their children had been a good decision.

Despite being warned it was a recipe for disaster, I'd opened this dance studio in a community where I knew no one. I'd trusted my gut and planted my roots. I'd graduated from college and then opened the business just weeks later, and it had felt right. It felt like home.

From the beginning, my advertising was bold: "We Do Dance Differently." *We,* so people wouldn't think it was just me. *Differently*, how? *Differently*, why? I couldn't wait to show them. During my very first open house, I'd sent home printed flyers and specialty mailers and wondered if anyone would actually show up.

And they did. First there was one, then five, then twenty, then fifty, then a hundred. And just like magic, the business was born.

Recital day had finally arrived. All the excitement and anticipation had led me to this moment. Today was about showing them. Proving to them. Exceeding their expectations. Creating not just a show but a show "unlike all others." A show that showcased amazing kids—their kids—kids with amazing potential. This show had become my obsession. A show with professional programs and scenery. A show that would transport the audience out of their neighborhood theater and into a world of the arts, performed by their little emerging artists. This was the day they would see how and why "We Do Dance Differently."

We had sold out the entire high school auditorium, and I was thrilled there was so much excitement for our very first big event.

I didn't sleep a wink the night before. The specialty T-shirts I had ordered never made it to the dress rehearsal, so I'd spent the morning driving all around town searching for the UPS truck. I'd finally spotted it about four miles from my location, signaled the driver to pull over to the side of the road, and grabbed my shirts.

Crisis averted.

Checking, double-checking, and triple-checking. The flowers, the programs, the costumes, the music, the tickets, the backstage helpers, the lighting designers, the ushers. Making sure everything was meticulous. Everything set, I headed to the theater.

When I walked in, I was overwhelmed by the smell of paint and mildew. I was confronted by the janitor, who informed me that the previous night's severe weather had caused extensive ceiling damage and some ceiling tiles had come crashing down, rendering a section of the auditorium uninhabitable.

"But the show is sold out," I told him.

We scrambled to clean up the area, block off the danger zone, throw away the debris, and add a new seating section.

Crisis averted.

The doors opened, and the auditorium began to fill. Lots of children milled around the backstage area, and the first group of dancers took their place on stage. The energy in the air was electric. My heart was beating so fast, I thought even the people in the last row of the theater would be able to see my chest heaving.

The curtain opened, the sound engineer pushed play, and I waited for the first song to start. Nothing. The dancers were in their pose, waiting. I grabbed a set of headphones and yelled into the headset mic, "MUSIC!" That's when the sound engineer told me the brand-new tape deck I had bought just a week before wasn't working. No music.

But I had a backup. My dance teacher mentor had trained me well, and I had placed a second tape recorder under the sound operator's desk. Within minutes, the auditorium was filled with music, and the children were dancing their hearts out.

Crisis averted.

The next few performances went off without a hitch, and the roar of applause filled the auditorium. It was happening. We were on our way.

It was about twenty minutes into the ninety-minute performance when I first spotted the fire marshal approaching as I was standing in the wings so I could see the kids on stage.

"Who's in charge?" he bellowed.

I raised my hand.

He was serious and direct. And although his pace was quick, everything that happened next I experienced in slow motion.

"We have an emergency," he said. "Someone has called in a bomb threat. We might need to evacuate."

(I think it's important to note here that this was well before 9/11, and the tragic events that have plagued our schools in recent memory were not even conceivable during this time.)

"It's probably just a prank," he said. "The junior high kids are having a social downstairs in the cafeteria, and this is how the upperclassmen get their kicks. But it's your call. Do you want us to do a sweep of the theater? We can help you navigate the chaos if you decide to call it quits."

It's my call... Navigate the chaos... Call it quits... I felt sick as his words swirled in my head.

All the hard work and sweat equity. All the anticipation. All the resources and expenses that had gone into this day. This one day. This day was supposed to put us on the map. This day was supposed to set our star trajectory. And now this.

Immediately, the entire day's events ran through my mind. The T-shirts, the crashing tiles, the brand-new music player. I'd navigated it all. I was quick and resilient and no one was the wiser, but would this be the straw that broke the camel's back?

So without thinking much about it, I grabbed a microphone and stepped out on stage. I was immediately welcomed with warm applause, which gave me the courage to speak.

"Thank you, everyone, for trusting me with your children… " I explained how the last ten months had been the most impactful of my life. "I do have something to share with you… " With full transparency, I reiterated what the fire marshal had shared with me, word for word, leaving nothing out. "I will fully reimburse anyone who's not comfortable staying, but I am making the decision to stay and dance." I wanted their support but completely understood their position if they decided to go and thanked them for the opportunity to serve them, regardless of their decision.

The show went on.

The business exploded that summer. The student numbers doubled and profits soared.

That very first show is one I will never forget, not because of the mishaps but because I became a business owner that day. From that day forward, I became their leader. I learned that although we work hard to achieve—although we have the will to exceed (and succeed)—there are still some things we just can't control. Even when we do things right, despite our best efforts, sometimes things just don't go as planned.

It isn't the uncertainty but how we navigate the uncertainty that matters—how we stay calm and consistent in times of chaos. It's in those moments that our will to move forward and our work ethic to persevere will carry us through the ebbs and flows of the entrepreneurial journey.

I learned that day that the people who can navigate the uncomfortable—the leaders who can stay consistent in the unexpected and the business owners who can prevail despite obstacles—will reach a level of success most will only dream of.

By the Way

Bomb scare on my very first recital. Okay, Universe, I see you. But it's okay. I've been preparing for this.

It's in My DNA

I grew up in a little house on the side of a minor highway, and the traffic was always loud. No matter the time of day, you couldn't escape the noise, and the house shook when the trucks drove by and generated mini earthquakes. It was a shabby two-bedroom house, and I shared a bedroom with my younger brother until I was about eleven years old. Everything in our home was a hand-me-down from someone, so nothing matched, which never really seemed to bother my parents. They weren't motivated by material objects, yet they spared no expense for my brother and me. I never wanted for anything. If money was tight, I never felt it. The house was worn down on the outside, but the inside was filled with love. I had two adoring parents who moved heaven and earth for the two kids they cherished.

When I was in the sixth grade, my parents made a big announcement: they were opening a business. My father was the entrepreneur in the family. He was an inventor and a visionary with big dreams. From as far back as I can remember, he was always thinking of ways to go into business for himself, but this was going to be the game changer—a small café. The American dream, right?

There were red flags right from the beginning. First, the location was sixty miles from our house. It wasn't long before the café became a drain on my parents—monopolizing money, time, and family. I'm not sure exactly when it happened, but what had started out as the American dream for my father quickly became a burden for my mother. She was the principal employee (actually the only employee), which meant working seven days a week, ten to twelve hours a day—a schedule she endured for the rest of my childhood.

I know I inherited my entrepreneurial *will* from my father, but I got my *work ethic* from my mother. My mother was tireless in her pursuit to serve her family. She never complained or wavered while she worked and worked and worked. She endured a three-hour commute for decades, even though it meant missing out on dance recitals and baseball games, school plays and family dinners.

It wasn't until years later that I truly recognized the sacrifice she had made for her family. She never really owned a business. She owned a job. Or should I say the job owned her? I vowed at a young age to take the lessons my parents instilled in me but to make better choices. I would choose to do the hard stuff better and make choices that aligned with the life I wanted to live, be stronger in my convictions, and above all else, live a life by design rather than by default.

My father had the *will* and my mother had the *work ethic*, and if I was ever going to be successful, I knew I needed both.

THE W'S IN YOUR WEALTH-OILED MACHINE: WILL AND WORK ETHIC

Not a Rat Race, but a Relay Race

Regardless of the industry, I have always thought of business not as a rat race but as a relay race. Someone hands me the baton—an inspiration, an idea, a concept—and I run with it. I have the baton now, so how fast can I run?

I don't believe the business exists *because of* me or *for* me. I believe it exists *through* me. The business comes through me like a child comes through me. It helps complete who I am, and it helps me feel a sense of purpose. I believe I was a conduit for my children. I know they don't belong to me. I was merely the vehicle that brought them into this world, and yet the sense of love, obligation, and responsibility is overwhelming. The same is true for business. Although I am just the vehicle, the businesses have healed me and helped me feel both satisfaction and significance.

WILL

Your will can't be predicated on the hopes, dreams, or aspirations of someone else. Your work ethic must drive you to do better and be better for no one but yourself.

Stephanie P. Kemp

People in my inner circle lovingly refer to me as "relentlessly focused." Was I born that way? From my earliest memory, I was driven. But I think *will* goes much deeper. Like a dog with a bone, when I become fixated on an inspiration or a path for new opportunities, my *will* remains "relentlessly focused."

A few years into owning my first business, I decided to purchase a new building. I had a strong will to create financial independence, so owning real estate and paying myself instead of the bank were top on my list of priorities. I spent over seven figures on a property in the next town over, only to learn months later that the building inspector was refusing access. Turns out the building commission didn't want my "little girl" business in their coveted business park. The easier path would have been to pack up, sell the building (for a profit), and move back to where I was wanted. But my *will* just wouldn't allow it. I remained undeterred. I stood on principle. I stood on the value I was creating for the community. I stood on the shoulders of the people who supported me. I stayed and fought. I fought and won.

Entrepreneurs who survive and thrive in business do so because their vision and *will* are steadfast. They have a fire that burns… fuels… moves… breaks through every challenge.

So, was I born with a strong will? The answer is absolutely. And I believe we all are. I believe all children are born with a will to persevere and overcome, and it is the fear they later develop that minimizes their dreams.

The next time you are in the presence of a young child learning to crawl, walk, and stretch for things out of their reach, consider their *will*. Consider their resolve. Consider their perseverance and determination. It's inspirational.

When my son was in the first grade, he came home from school with a gingerbread house he'd made in class. The second he walked in the door, his two-year-old sister wanted nothing else.

She was relentless in her pursuit, and after a dozen failed attempts, we did what we thought was in everyone's best interest—we put the gingerbread house on top of the refrigerator. We figured "out of sight, out of mind," but that didn't deter my strong-willed toddler. As soon as the coast was clear, she moved the kitchen chair over to the counter, climbed over to the cabinet door, and swung herself up on top of the refrigerator.

Imagine my surprise when I rounded the corner into our kitchen and found my two-year-old eating shellacked gumdrops on top of our refrigerator.

Strong-willed?! Strong-willed was an understatement.

As a teacher, I can recognize a student's will almost instantly. It's the look that speaks without words. It's absolute determination. It's hardwired. They know they are meant to do something great, something different, something meaningful.

I have also witnessed foundations and scholarships created because a person's *will* compelled them to create something better, something for others, something bigger than themselves.

Some of us never lose our childlike will. But those who lost it can find it and rekindle it once again when the *want* is great enough and when the fear of not doing becomes far greater than the fear of failure.

WORK ETHIC

Talent is cheaper than table salt. What separates the talented individual from the successful one is hard work.

Stephen King

Some people are born with amazing talents, but I have seen firsthand that the people whose values are centered around the importance of work ethic and determination are the people changing the world.

I believe I was born with talents, but I've trained my gifts. I believe I was born a teacher, but I trained to become a mentor. I believe I was born an entrepreneur, but I trained to become a business owner. I believe I was born a woman, but I trained to become a wife. I believe I was born a female, but I trained to become a mother.

Having the will to train means understanding I am the steward of my craft. I have a responsibility to those that came before me and an obligation to those who will come after me. I have a responsibility to preserve the integrity of the original form while still innovating and expanding on new principles.

I recite the following to myself as part of my daily routine. I wrote it over twenty years ago, but even after all these years, it still inspires me to get up each day and win.

Run, Stephanie, run. I have the baton now, so I will run like the wind. I will run to beat the time—to persevere. I have the baton now, and I will continue to run in hopes of making the ones who came before me proud. I have the baton now, and I will continue to run until it is time for me to pass the baton to the next person waiting in line.

For me, hard work is always the expectation, so although I don't reward hard work, I do reward results. Results for a sustained work ethic—a work ethic that understands the importance of execution.

If I hire someone to do a project, I want that project done on time. I want that project to exceed my expectations, not once, but always. I am not considering how "hard" they worked. I only consider the results.

The same is true when I'm on the receiving end. No one should care how hard I work. No one should care about the effort or the time invested. They should measure the results. They should measure what is delivered.

Being efficient and working smarter is an essential key to creating a wealth-oiled machine. Having the mindset that a work ethic must sustain and consistently strive for excellence without falling victim to overwhelm and burden is essential.

How do I do that? I choose my projects carefully, and I create systems that help me produce consistent results. I set expectations to match reality, so I am not crumbling under arbitrary pressures. I do what I say I'm going to do, every time. I show up on time, and I keep my commitments. I build a support system around me to help me achieve successful outcomes.

In my wealth-oiled machine, it is important that my will and work ethic stay in alignment because my roles as entrepreneur, CEO, mentor, teacher, coach, wife, and mother are far too important to have fatigue, stress, and burnout as part of my job description.

How about You?

What would you do if your *will* to succeed and your *work ethic* to exceed were no longer in alignment? How would you keep getting up and persevering if you'd lost your spark and enthusiasm?

I have seen the frustration and pitfalls that entrepreneurs face when their *will* and *work ethic* are out of balance. Having one without the other can cause burnout and fatigue and even failure. I have witnessed too many visionaries with amazing ideas lose momentum because they lacked the stick-to-itiveness necessary to navigate their entrepreneurial vision.

I understand that feeling uninspired can affect one's productivity, creativity, and overall well-being. So let's look at how you can get your mojo back if you ever feel discouraged.

First, it's important to identify the root cause of your listless motivation. Is it a lack of challenge or conviction? Are you afraid of failure? Are you stuck or stagnant? Do you feel there are limited growth opportunities? Are you navigating poor relationships? Do you have a purpose behind the motivation?

It's essential to understand the purpose behind the motivation because it's the motivation that will get you up each day feeling excited about seeking new opportunities. It's the motivation that will carry a strong, sustained work ethic. It's the motivation that becomes your *will*. Once you understand your true will and why your work ethic supports it, there will be no limit to the success you can achieve.

I would never have achieved my successful life if I hadn't been completely clear about why it needed to exist in my life—in my life and not somebody else's.

Initially, I didn't think about making a difference in the world; I just wanted to do something a lot of other people were doing but do it a whole lot better. So my motivation was to prove to myself and everyone around me that I could sustain a level of success. I could raise the bar, set higher expectations, and hold everyone accountable. I could create a standard of achievement that was consistent and measurable. I could survive on top—not just be successful, but stay successful, stay inspired, and maintain a level of excellence that exceeded expectations.

So your motivation doesn't need to be a big philosophical "change the world" agenda. Your motivation may be to make more money, or share a talent, provide a solution, or inspire the next generation. Or it may be to do something everyone else is doing but do it better. Like a professional athlete determined to become the absolute best at one extraordinary skill, you have to find that one thing that motivates you to reach for more. There is no right or wrong answer—the point is only that the answer is yours.

Your *will* will constantly be tested, and if you don't have a clear driver, if you aren't clear on your purpose, your motivation may not endure. And without that will, the holes may be too deep and your resolve may succumb to the overwhelm.

So answering this one question today may bring you closer to your objective: What is the one thing that moves you to persevere despite challenges? If you can answer that, you will have defined your *will.*

The economy will ebb and flow, a pandemic may again raise its ugly head, banks will continue to crash, you will have an unruly customer, and the neighborhood building inspector may never recognize your value. What then?

How will your *will* respond? If obstacles easily deter you or you find it difficult to muster up the motivation to sustain a high *work ethic*, then most likely your will and work ethic are not aligned.

That is the key—the key to your will and work ethic alignment in a wealth-oiled machine.

So how do you become aligned? Instead of making a list of excuses, create a list of beliefs. Turn those beliefs into actions. The best part of being an entrepreneur is designing the life you want to live. Your life and not somebody else's.

For me, true alignment occurred when I had the courage to do, say, and live my life based on what I believed to be true, even when it was controversial and even when I was afraid of what others would think about me. I found that even when I was keeping an eye on my long-term mission and continuing to set new goals, even when I was training and learning and growing while surrounded by like-minded people, even when I aligned my personal and professional objectives, they were still only short-term solutions—short-term solutions if I didn't have the motivation to support my *will.* So the list of beliefs became my reality. I was clear as to why they existed. They weren't just *important* to me; they were my oxygen.

The frustrations, the failures, the falls, and the holes are guaranteed—the success is not.

I get asked all the time how I know if a business idea or concept will be successful. The simple answer is I don't, so I only move forward when the *fear* of not doing it outweighs the *fear* of taking action. Whether it's pain or joy or fear or love, when the motivation is great enough, we all move. For me, it was always the fear—the fear of not doing enough, the fear of not reaching my full potential, the fear of not squeezing every last bit of opportunity out of whatever I was committed to.

So what will you choose? Will you choose to stay safe, choose to stay stuck, or choose more?

When my *will* and *work ethic* are in alignment, it's because my purpose and motivation are in alignment. So it becomes easier for me to enhance my skill development, create new pathways, open new opportunities, and commit to long-term decisions.

I have never been relentlessly focused on a task, a job, a skill, or an outcome that didn't *matter* to me. I am not interested in information for information's sake. But if the information and education support my purpose and motivation, I won't stop learning and I won't be denied.

There was a time when you couldn't crawl, pull up, or walk, and a time when things were beyond your reach, but your *will* and *work ethic* persevered. There was a time when you weren't afraid to ask for help. There was a time when your will and work ethic were aligned, so you were resilient and undeterred.

You may not remember that time, but you have always had the power. You had the strength to lift yourself up, and you had the courage to reach for someone's hand. You were born with all the will and work ethic you will ever need in this life. It lives within you. You just need to reach down deep and spark it.

NOTES

CHAPTER 2

EXPECTATIONS AND EQUITY

Apples and Oranges

The mother of our latest prospective student was determined to make the right choice for her five-year-old daughter, who bounced enthusiastically at her side as she toured our studio.

"How do you 'do dance differently'?" she asked. "All the dance studios look and sound the same. What makes yours unique? At her age, does it really matter where she starts to dance?"

I loved this question. My answer was the reason I'd started this business in the first place.

"I believe it does make a difference, and here's why… " and I proceeded to tell her the story of Jenny.

I was on a college audition tour when I met eighteen-year-old Jenny and her mom on a crowded train. My hair in a bun and my dance bag slung over my shoulder, they must have suspected we were heading to the same place because they made room for me to join them. I was thankful for the invitation because the train was overbooked, and without their kindness, I could have been standing for the majority of the four-hour ride into New York City.

It took less than an hour for me to learn all about Jenny and her entire dance history. She'd been dancing since she was two. Never took a break. Six days a week. No other activities. Private lessons on top of a rigorous schedule. And her favorite dance genre was ballet. Her dream, since she was six, was to dance at New York University (NYU). Every Christmas, she dragged her entire family (including her three brothers) to see the Rockettes just so she could walk around the NYU campus. Man, she was committed! With every bated breath, I could feel her excitement. The anticipation of this moment didn't seem too big for her. She was giddy, excited, and full of life.

I was far less enthusiastic. The audition at NYU was known to be grueling. The acceptance rate was low. I'd taken a year off from training, and ballet was not my genre of choice. Petite with a strong athletic build, I looked more like a gymnast than a ballerina, and I was immediately second-guessing my decision to audition. But I was doing it for my mother. The woman who had worked tirelessly to give me every dance opportunity had urged me to go, so there I was.

I asked Jenny if she'd prepared an allegro or an adagio for her solo presentation and was surprised by her hesitation and blank expression. In fact, she looked like a deer caught in the headlights. Was she unsure of the question? Or maybe she just didn't want to share? She looked to her mother for guidance and then sluffed off the question. I didn't press it. She was the one who hadn't taken a break from dance. She was the one who had sacrificed all other activities. She was the one who had invested in private lessons. I was just coming off a year hiatus. I was the one juggling dance and cheer and theater and track. Who was I to judge?

When the conductor announced our stop, we disembarked and walked the eight minutes to our final destination together. Or I should say, I walked and Jenny skipped. Once we got on site, Jenny and I went one way while her mom (after taking two dozen pictures) headed to the designated area where she would wait for us.

Jenny was very talkative and loud as we entered the building, but the vibe there was anything but jubilant. You could cut the tension with a knife. So I went into deep audition mode while Jenny continued to flutter around the locker room, introducing herself to everyone she met.

The company director made a quick announcement, collected our solo tapes for the final leg of the audition, and handed us each a number. Jenny and I weren't in the same group, so I gave her a hug and wished her luck. We agreed to meet afterward, and I made my way through the studio doors.

Sitting in the back of the room, I understood exactly why Jenny had given me a blank stare when I'd asked her the question on the train.

Jenny was not prepared for this audition. She didn't even make it through the beginning barre combinations. After about twenty minutes, the director discreetly handed her back her solo tape and walked her out. I was devastated for her.

The audition lasted another three hours, and by the time I got out, Jenny was nowhere to be found. She wasn't on the same train back, and I never saw her again. But I think of her often.

"Jenny is the reason I opened my dance studio," I told the young mother with her little dancer bouncing at her side. "What should Jenny have done differently? What should her studio have done differently? Jenny had sacrificed. Jenny had put in the sweat equity. Jenny had been committed—far more committed than I. Jenny's family had sacrificed and invested. What had gone wrong?" I let the questions hang between us for a moment. "I wasn't naive to the dance studio model. I knew there were no regulations or certifications for opening a dance studio. I knew there were no 'standards of excellence,' and yet the thought that a studio got this so wrong baffled me. What if Jenny's mom had chosen another dance studio when Jenny was just two? Would the trajectory of Jenny's life be completely different today?"

I smiled at the mother and her enthusiastic little girl and gave her my heartfelt answer. "We give every single child access to the best teachers we can find, and we expect our teachers and students to teach and reach for excellence. Your daughter will have a lot of fun here, but she will also set goals, work hard, and be held accountable to herself and her peers. Our expectation is that every child receives the opportunity to fully express their potential."

The Decision to Reach for Excellence

When I was in ninth grade, I decided to take a break from everything. I traded in the lead role in the school play for a pack of new friends and my dance shoes for a pack of cigarettes and said so long to my old life. No schedule, no practices, no job, no care, no responsibility. Some kids made hanging out after school look glamorous, so I decided to give it a try. What did I have to lose?

The problem was that it was hard work failing: keeping up with the lies, cutting corners, scheduling the non-schedule, navigating the new relationships, and cutting classes. It was exhausting. My grades didn't slip—they plummeted. At some point during the year, my parents asked about a report card, and I told them report cards had been cut because of new school budgets. Of course they believed me. I was a great actress, and up until this point, I had been a good student, so why would I lie?

I kept up the charade until the middle of the fourth term when my guidance counselor called my house. Normally, that would have been a nonissue, as both my parents worked long hours and were never home to answer the phone. However, on this particular day, my father had gotten home early. It seemed like a curse, but I later recognized it as a blessing. The jig was up. I was caught, and my days of underachieving were over.

It wasn't long before I was sitting in a hot classroom, waiting to get extra help with the same algebra problems that had sent me to summer school in the first place. (Yeah, I ended up in summer school.) The summer school math class was three hours each morning, and as if three hours of algebra wasn't punishment enough, I'd been staying after class every day for extra help. Math was a struggle for me. What was basic and common sense for many was NASA-level stuff for me.

As I approached the desk and started to pull out my textbook, my teacher turned away from me and very nonchalantly spoke under his breath, "Ahh, you again. Don't worry about this. You're cute. You'll get a husband."

This response was not completely out of character in the eighties, and I didn't take offense. The teacher meant no malice. But at that very moment, the challenge was issued and my competitive spirit was reignited.

Was this how he saw me? Was this his expectation of me? I mean, we were only five days into a six-week session. Had he already made up his mind about my potential?

I walked the long way home that day after school and found myself not at my house but at my neighbor's. She was three years older and a math whiz. I knocked on the door and asked her if she would be willing to tutor me. I'd been making $2.25 an hour (before I'd quit) and offered her $2.00 an hour to help me. When she agreed, I immediately called to get my job back, and we worked together every afternoon for the next six weeks.

What I realized in that summer school math class was that although $|x-a|= a^2-x^2$ was never going to serve me, I still had to figure out a way to be successful. Despite the challenges, despite the shortcomings, from that day forward, I wasn't willing to double down on anything that wouldn't propel my life forward. I could continue to take the path of least resistance, I could wallow in my lack of natural skill or blame others for my failures, or I could expect more. I could continue to work at being mediocre, or I could commit to working at being successful. The choice was mine.

So, despite all odds, I got an A in that algebra summer class, but not because I became a strong math student. On the contrary. I just understood I needed to create a system that would help me be successful. I don't always have the information, and I certainly don't always have the answers. But since that day, I've always had the determination to expect more. I kept that summer school A as a reminder to never let anyone underestimate me again.

By the Way

I ran into that math teacher years later, and I remember thinking, *Yes, you were right. I was cute and I did get a husband, but I was also a successful CEO and millionaire before I hit thirty. And maybe more importantly, I never used* $|x-a|= a^2-x^2$ *to get there, not even once.*

The E's in Your Wealth-Oiled Machine: Expectations and Equity

A Leg in the Relay Race

In the dance industry, some would argue that dance as art should not be confused with business. That dance should be a safe space for self-expression, building life skills, forming community, and finding joy through movement—not predicated on making money. There is also the camp that believes that dance, unlike a team sport, should not be judged and that each organization should set its own rules and standards. If you agree with either of these completely, then we may be at a crossroads, but if you are ready to challenge these beliefs, please keep reading.

I struggle with this discrepancy in the dance industry—in any industry, really. Where does the learning of historical data factor in as a baseline? If we are teaching lessons, isn't English, English? Isn't biology, biology? Isn't dance, dance? If dance education is something that has been handed down to us, aren't we then the stewards? Aren't we just one leg in the relay race?

In the dance industry, I understand that most children won't aspire to a career in the performing arts. Most children will walk through the doors of a dance studio or any other business that caters to children because they're looking for fun and social connection. But what if every child were still offered the same level of opportunity, the same level of instruction, the same level of care and excellence? What if every child, despite their natural talent, despite their level of commitment, despite their body type, or their financial investment, were taught the same lessons and held to the same standards?

These were my questions: Could all children be held to their own individual level of excellence—taught empowering lessons and given opportunities to rise—even if that meant losing, falling short, or being disappointed? Was there a way to create a safe space for self-expression, build life skills, form community, and not just survive, but thrive financially?

Could the short-term disappointments be leveraged? Could the potential for success be heightened, not in spite of the bumps but because of them?

Most importantly, was there a way to mitigate the risk of more Jennys?

EXPECTATIONS

No one rises to low expectations.

Les Brown

For entrepreneurs and those they lead and serve, the role of expectations cannot be overstated, but who decides the trajectory of education? And if we decide to market those lessons, charge for services, what then is our duty and responsibility to the people we are called to serve? How do we help educate our prospective clients on what they are, in fact, buying? How do we establish a standard of excellence in an industry, in every industry, that compels businesses to do better and be better for the people in our community, locally or globally?

Financial freedom while reinventing the traditional dance studio model—that was my expectation. I wanted to celebrate the beginner dancer and the advanced dancer in a way that honored both of them, that challenged both of them. I wanted to hold each student and teacher accountable. I wanted to thrive financially without compromising on quality. I wanted to not just get to the top but stay on top. And I wanted to give each student the opportunity to reach their goals—each student, regardless of what was "expected" of them.

I have had the privilege of working with thousands of children at every level—from the very beginner to the top dancers in the country. Children are made in all shapes and sizes. Some are naturally talented and others work for every accolade. I'm grateful for the small role I have played in helping children realize their dreams, no matter where those dreams direct them, dance or otherwise. I never presume to know the path, and I never count any child out. I believe all people have the capability to set high expectations and rise.

As leaders, what is our responsibility if we can't guarantee results? In a product-based business, we list ingredients, so how do we maintain quality control when what we're selling is subjective? How do we grade ourselves if we're creating a product or service in any industry, whether it be a better mousetrap or a new product altogether? And does our perception of value match what our customers are expected to pay?

I believe as entrepreneurs, we should be relentlessly focused on creating impact, challenging the norms, and reinventing the status quo. I believe it is our responsibility to encourage everyone in our organization to look beyond past limitations. To help people see obstacles not as a negative, but instead as a tool to help propel them forward. I work tirelessly to create community and unity so that the people in my circle will not only strive to meet expectations but *exceed* them.

I don't want anyone under my watch to believe there are any limits on what they can achieve. I believe people are born with endless possibilities, and it is the fear they later develop that minimizes them. Keep exposing them to greatness, and they will become great. Surround them with leaders, and they will lead. If you want someone on your watch to achieve great things, expect it.

By the Way

One of my very first students had the aim of dancing at NYU. She came to me a little late in her development, so she worked her tail off, but her dream came true. She received a master's degree from NYU and went on to receive her PhD. This reinforced my position that children are born with endless possibilities, and as educators, it is our duty to help them set the bar high and persevere.

That one's for you, Jenny!

EQUITY

The difference between equity and equality is that equality is everyone gets the same thing and equity is everyone gets the things they deserve.

DeRay Mckesson

There has been a strong push in recent years to level the playing field. Make life "even." Stop keeping score and create different paths for achievement.

This "everyone gets a trophy" philosophy is, in my opinion, hurting us.

I am a successful business owner, coach, teacher, and mentor because I persevered. It wasn't talent, money, or luck that got me here. It was my *resolve*. Every time I got knocked down, I got back up… again, and again, and again. Those lessons are what strengthened my character. The motto "Don't Ask for It, Work for It" is, in fact, my company's theme song. If I'd had an easier road, I might have been sheltered from some disappointments, but that protection also would have kept me from living up to my potential.

When we level people in sports, in competitions, in tournaments, in showcases, we teach them it is all about the trophy and not about the resilience to work hard and persevere. We risk depriving them of the opportunity to reach their full potential, as well as potentially undermining them in front of their peers.

Instead of chasing the championship trophy, what if all our energy went into chasing the championship performance? The championship performance in all aspects of our life.

I was called to this earth to stand with children and, more recently, with fellow entrepreneurs, because I believe they are capable of more. I believe people should learn about adversity, obstacles, and challenges in a safe space so that later in life they have the tools to navigate disappointments with courage and grace.

The truth is, the odds of failure are high, so the win in skill development, experience, and character becomes far more valuable. If we don't learn these lessons when we're young, when should we expect to learn them?

Are we still at a crossroads? If you are still on the fence about where your business stands, then I ask you to consider this: If you run ads. If you vie for market share. If you charge for lessons or services. If you fight to retain customers. If you seek education and resources to gain an advantage in your business. If you do any or all of these things, then you are a competitor. Then you own a competitive business and you have learned to persevere and take risks, even when those risks have led to disappointments, even when they led to losses. The rest is simply semantics.

So if we understand the nature of competition. If we understand life is, in fact, a competition. If we understand our success is not the result of someone else's failure and that ultimately the only person we should be competing against is ourselves, then why wouldn't we pass those life lessons on to the next generation? If we continue to teach children that they can "opt out" and take the easier path for instant gratification, why would we assume they would "stay in" and persevere as adults when the going gets tough?

It's not the fact that people will experience loss that keeps me up at night. It's the fact that we are creating a generation of people who will never experience the true joy of the win. The win that is earned and not just handed to them, the only win that will, in fact, have the power to change them.

How About You?

Do you believe it's imperative that you set the bar high and encourage the people around you to persevere? Are you willing to endure short-term sacrifices for long-term achievement? Do you agree that setting high expectations alone is not enough, but that those around you understand they must be willing to earn their reward?

I know from experience that setting the bar high can be daunting, especially when you fall short or others miss the mark.

One of my biggest struggles is working through disappointments. The disappointments that come when vendors miss deadlines or customers are dissatisfied with a product or service that I have spent sweat equity creating.

I remember the first time a client fired me for not being transparent about expectations. She believed as a new business owner, I lacked the pedigree or track record to justify the mission and vision for my new venture. So despite my best efforts, she left. I was sick over it. It was certainly a blow to my ego. I worried about not being talented enough or smart enough. I wondered if I had the thick skin to persevere in such a personal business, a business that is ultimately built on relationships.

But the truth was, we weren't the right fit, so firing me was the right decision. I wasn't going to change my mindset, my culture, or my expectations, and her objectives weren't in line with my company's vision. She wasn't my ideal client because we weren't like-minded, and there was a clear discrepancy between our expectations and our realities.

So the real issue wasn't about where I set the bar, or my expectations. The real issue was about how those expectations were communicated. I hadn't properly communicated my non-negotiables, and that's why the relationship fell apart.

I quickly learned the importance of not only setting expectations but also being transparent about them. I quickly realized it wasn't about changing the *minds* of my customers to make things fit; it was about finding like-*minded* customers who shared my philosophies.

Open communication throughout the organization became key, so everyone who worked with me in any capacity understood I would never take the path of least resistance—not for myself and not for them.

If I kept lowering the bar based on my customers, employees, staff, clients, friends, or partners, then I risked never meeting or exceeding expectations at all.

So instead, I set the bar high in my personal and professional life and worked through challenges to help everyone rise. I was up-front about limitations and transparent about non-negotiables, and I leveraged perceived weaknesses. Inexperience was my calling card for taking risks, bringing fresh perspectives, and injecting a new energy or a new enthusiasm into a stale environment.

Limitations can quickly be leveraged if you are passionate about change, if you have the desire to learn and adapt to new challenges, seek opportunities for development, and build a network of guidance and support.

When I opened my first business, I didn't see my lack of experience as a disadvantage or challenge. I didn't set the bar low due to comparison—comparison between myself and the more experienced professionals. In my eyes, my lack of previous ownership didn't constitute a lack of potential or skill. I doubled down on the skills that would leverage my knowledge. Instead of being the expert at everything, I concentrated on being the expert at one thing—one thing, so when I spoke, people listened.

Expectations and *equity* are keys to your very own wealth-oiled machine, and transparency is the oil that keeps the gears churning. Transparency will help you define your goals—goals that are specific and measurable.

Once you have those goals, communicate your expectations and non-negotiables clearly and consistently and then lead by example.

Create a standard of excellence that obligates *you* to do better, be better, for the people you are called to serve.

When the people around you exceed your expectations, recognize and reward their success. When they don't, be quick to address the issue while always keeping the bar set high.

For my businesses, hard work is the expectation—*The Universal Language.*

"Good enough" cannot live in my personal or professional life. I believe we should be more responsible for what we sell and more diligent about quality control. Most importantly, I believe we must empower the people around us to play full-out and earn their way.

No doubt, you will have more challenges if you set the bar high. But what's the alternative? The alternative is not an option for me. So I navigate the disappointments and challenges. I am compassionate but not emotional in my business, so that always makes the tough conversations a little easier to navigate. I'm direct and emotionally regulated when I handle a conflict, and I never push anything to the side. I address it head-on. If you work for me, then you know going in that the bar is set high. So if we need to address a situation, I always address it *with the bar set high.*

I don't have the luxury of picking and choosing the opportunities to lead. I lead by example. I lead with consistency. I take full responsibility for any miscommunication or lack of support. If I have not set someone up for success in any capacity in my business, then I have failed them. *I have failed them.* So I'm quick to apologize and take full responsibility. Sometimes we come to a crossroads and need to part ways, but it's never done in the heat of the moment, and it's never done without thoughtful consideration. I started the business to build relationships, not destroy them, so that is always top of mind in any decision-making process, even when it's difficult.

If you want someone on your watch to achieve greatness, expect it and then model it.

You will inspire those around you to achieve more because they will have earned the respect and recognition *they deserve.*

When I empowered the people around me to earn their positions. When I threw away the path of mediocrity, the path of underachieving. When I held everyone to the same standards of excellence, I opened more doors for opportunity.

Every individual has their own path to follow. It's not always going to look the same. Even when given the same resources and opportunities, people will grow and develop in their own unique ways. Does that mean there will be winners and losers? Most certainly. Does that mean we then shy away from teaching people to persevere despite the obstacles? I don't believe so. Because one person's journey is no less valuable or important. The goal is to support and encourage all individuals regardless of where they are in their journey, even when they lose.

When I talk to parents about setting expectations for their children in any capacity that measures their growth and development, I often use this analogy:

I believe people are like tomato plants. They will ripen at different times, even when they're all planted at the same time. Although they receive the same amount of sun and we continue to water, feed, and weed them daily, the outcomes for each plant may still look different. Some will grow to different heights, and they will produce fruit at different times. So we keep the soil rich so each plant has the best opportunity to rise.

NOTES

CHAPTER 3

AIM AND ACCOUNTABILITY

Do Things Differently

I was three years into scaling and growing my business when I decided to hire my very first team member. I was also newly married and wanted a dedicated night off for date night. I didn't want to fall into the never-ending work trap my mother had endured for twenty years—the trap that would eventually lead to the dissolution of my parents' marriage. A marriage I had once looked up to and admired. A marriage I thought would stand the test of time.

So protecting my new marriage and building a team-managed company became my number one priority.

I placed an ad in the local paper and patiently waited. Nothing. Now when I say nothing, it isn't to say people didn't apply, but the "right" people didn't apply.

In walked "Polly." Polly was a dream candidate. Her résumé was impeccable. A professional ballerina. A principal dancer with the New York City Ballet. She held a master's degree in pedagogy and dance education. She had a ton of teaching experience with all levels of students. She had worked as a company director and as a professional choreographer. Hallelujah! My prayers were answered, or so I thought. Polly was perfect on paper, but something was missing. There was something missing that I learned later I couldn't live without.

In the beginning, my hiring process was a series of trials and errors. The most talented instructors weren't necessarily the best teachers, and some of the strong teachers didn't have the skill set necessary to be successful long-term. So learning about each candidate and creating a blueprint of an ideal team member was really important. A résumé could tell me what a person did, but a résumé couldn't tell me *who* a person was; and for me, who a person *is* became far more important.

It couldn't be about just filling a spot or position. I couldn't just plug a hole or create a placeholder. Every hire had to be the right person. My focus turned from filling the bus to making sure the right people were in the right seats on the bus.

So I threw away the job descriptions, the ad copy, and the contracts and started asking just one question of every potential candidate: "Are you committed to excellence?"

If the answer was a "hell yes," then we were on the right track.

I was committed to "doing things differently," so I needed talented, forward-thinking individuals who could help me light the path. It was an unorthodox approach—no job description, no contract, no noncompete—but it's the approach that has served me well.

In my studio, there was no recreational path for students—only an educational one—so every talented teacher had to teach every student. Of course, I wasn't expecting every student who walked through the door to be the next Mikhail Baryshnikov or Gregory

Hines, but I wanted each student to be given the same level of attention. Our mission centered around making sure each child had the very best support, guidance, training, and encouragement possible. No matter where their journey took them, beginner dancer or Miss World of Dance, we were going to give them our best.

So my first "right" hire took quite a while. I needed someone who didn't just aim but aimed high. Someone who wasn't just going to fulfill a job but was going to help me build a culture and a lifestyle. Someone who wasn't just working toward a paycheck but toward a future for themselves, our students, and the business. Someone who didn't just have the right skill set but also held themselves accountable.

I was looking for *me*.

As I grew my team, I surrounded myself with people I liked. People who had the same mindset that I had. People who took direction but could work independently. People who would support and grow my students. People who loved collaboration but set their own goals. People who didn't need to be micromanaged. People who would aim high every day, every month, every year, regardless of who was watching.

I surrounded myself with "high performers." I surrounded myself with others who shared the same love of excellence.

Setting My Sights

The A in algebra at the end of my ninth-grade year was the beginning of choosing the path of living into my potential, so I decided to head back into the dance classroom. Part of the resistance the year before was linked to the training facility being almost an hour away. Getting there with two working parents had presented quite the challenge. This time, I wanted to find something closer, a place within walking or bike-riding distance. Unfortunately, most of the local studios didn't offer the challenging classes I needed.

When I heard about a new studio that had opened not far from where I lived and was invited to one of their summer performances, I went to check it out. I definitely enjoyed the performance, but not as much as the intermission. At intermission, a sixteen-year-old boy I vaguely recognized from my high school came out to sweep the stage, and I was immediately overcome with déjà vu. This feeling that I didn't just know him but knew him well, even though we had never met. My heart raced and my palms got sweaty as the thought crossed my mind, *I'm going to marry that boy someday.*

Upon further investigation, I learned that this young man was the cousin of the studio director, and it was likely he'd be hanging around the dance studio because his sister danced there. That was all the convincing I needed. I signed up for classes the very next day, and seven years later, I married that boy.

And he was just the beginning. Every time I set my sights on something, I created a vision. Pursuing my dreams became about setting clear goals that were specific and measurable. I didn't worry about whether they were achievable; I only cared about whether they were relevant to my future. There was no timeline for the sacrifice because I was looking for long-term success and I stayed focused on the things that moved me forward. I broke down the goals into smaller bite-sized pieces, so I could stay accountable and track my progress. I created a plan that outlined steps for identifying potential obstacles and then devised strategies to overcome them. I shared my dreams with others so they could provide support and motivation—support but not permission. That was imperative because I looked for advice and guidance from people who were always one step ahead of me, even if they were outside my inner circle. Even if I never met them personally, I took their advice. And then, more importantly, I took action. I learned from my failures, which kept me motivated to keep striving. To continue striving for opportunity.

First it was the boy. Then it was opening my first business, second business, third business. The principles stayed the same, and the steps to creating a wealth-oiled machine were starting to develop: *W*in each day, *E*xpect more, *A*ction over procrastination, *L*ook forward, *T*ouch my best, follow my *H*eart.

I always believed the American Dream was within my grasp, but I never believed it was a given. And I certainly never thought I was entitled to success. I wanted to live a rich life—a *wealthy* life—so I needed to take advantage of opportunities when they presented themselves and make the most of every chance I got.

The A's in Your Wealth-Oiled Machine: Aim and Accountability

Get Some Sleep

Even though I've never participated in any organized sports, I'm fascinated by sports analogies and often use them to think about how I relate to my *aim* and *accountability* with my team.

For example, I am the quarterback of my business.

Why the quarterback? Because sometimes the quarterback is in every play, and sometimes the quarterback isn't even on the field. Regardless of where this pivotal player is, the team is always playing to win. I want that team mindset in my business. Keep moving the ball down the field, getting us closer to the goal post, with every snap, with every play.

Let's say my team is in a huddle and I've just called the play. The clock is ticking, and I need to get the ball into the hands of my receiver so we can score. I get the snap and see my receiver is wide open, so I throw the long ball. But my pass is off the mark. It's a bad throw—completely misses the intended target. And because of my inept pass, we lose the game.

Now, you may be thinking, "Well, you're the boss. No one is going to fire you. You don't need to answer to anyone. Better luck next time." But the truth is, when I underperform, when I don't play to my full potential, I'm sick over it. Even after all these years, I hold myself accountable for every play. And if I fail, I won't sleep for days because of it. I will rerun the play over and over in my mind. *How did this happen? What should I have done differently? How can I prepare better in the future?*

My obsession with replay is the direct result of being a high performer. I compete with one person—myself. I won't sleep until I have the opportunity to prove myself again.

That's why I have to surround myself with other high performers. Not only do they make me better, push me to be better, challenge me to do better, but they also do something else for me that is far more important—they allow me to sleep.

Despite the fact that I train every day to get better, I still fumble sometimes and have to surround myself with highly skilled people who can catch my flubs.

I think about the times I overbooked schedules, had one too many "great ideas," didn't do an adequate job onboarding, or invested in costly software… not in English.

Although making mistakes and fumbling the ball is a natural part of the learning process, it softens the blow when you have the right people in the right place ready to catch the ball when you throw a bad pass.

So I empowered the people around me to be independent thinkers. I wanted to support them but still allow them the freedom they needed to make decisions on the fly.

Now, let's say my team is in a huddle and I have just called a play. The clock is ticking, and I need to get the ball into the hands of my receiver so we can score. I get the snap, see my receiver is wide open, and throw the long ball. This time, it's a beautiful throw—perfect throw—right into the hands of my receiver. But the receiver drops the ball. They fumble.

Do you know who's up all night tossing and turning? *They are.* They're running the replay over and over in their head. *How did this happen? What should I have done differently? How can I prepare better in the future?* And… I'm sleeping like a baby.

Now you may be thinking, come on, it's not that easy. The buck stops with the business owner, and as the leader of any organization, it's tough to get a good night's sleep when the team is fumbling. *Touché!* That's true, but the lesson is in the expectation that any successful team must be invested in the outcomes because together, we set goals, we aim higher, we push forward, we fall, we lose sleep, we learn, we do better, and we win.

AIM

The greatest danger for most of us is not that our aim [expectation] is too high and we miss it, but that it is too low and we reach it.

Michelangelo

I heard once that our childhood either changes who we are or solidifies it. Although there's a lot about my childhood I wouldn't change, the things that have been the most impactful in my life have resulted from the things I was willing to do differently. I didn't just follow the leader—I aimed higher. I didn't focus on the common or expected—I expected more.

For me, the success of owning a business was never about getting to the top; it was about surviving on top. It was never about being successful but rather about staying successful. It was never about having more but about keeping more.

My success came from deciding on the life I wanted before it even existed and knowing that each decision would either propel me forward or backward. So I chose wisely. I made decisions that were in alignment with my life. I didn't wake up one day and think, *Wow, how did this happen?* It was planned step by step, decision by decision.

When I started out, I was a solo entrepreneur. I taught every class myself. I was the head teacher, choreographer, office manager, janitor, customer service representative, marketer, sales director, and editor. I wasn't afraid of the long hours. I thrived on it all. I wanted to refine the skill set, I wanted to get the culture right. I wanted to create a culture before I created a brand. I wanted to become an expert in my business. I wanted my hands on everything that came through the business so I could learn and grow.

I focused on growing the business and building community, and I was constantly seeking new opportunities to expand my reach and increase my resources. But I quickly learned the difference between growth and scale when it became impossible for me to keep all the balls in the air.

I could continue to add growth and increase revenue, but if I wanted to scale, if I wanted to create a real impact, if I wanted to expand my vision and my mission, I had to replace myself… with myself.

Scaling and growing my businesses with others who aim high has allowed me to continue to love my work, create lifelong impact, honor my employees, support my community, build wealth, and most importantly, grow a healthier branch on my family tree.

I worked hard when I was at work and played hard when I was at home. I am a high performer, but not a perfectionist or a micromanager, so I was never pulled into the weeds of the day-to-day operations. I surrounded myself with people who prided themselves on the job they were doing. We were accountable to each other, but more importantly, everyone who worked for me was accountable to all our students, the families we served, and the unique culture we were building.

When I surrounded myself with highly skilled high performers, I got to build a team-managed company. I developed a company that understood how to win, regardless of who was watching. I assembled a team that was accountable to themselves and to each other. I built a team that consistently aimed high.

I realized the power of this model when I was leaving for a long weekend right after one of my first hires. One of my first employees yelled out behind me, "Have fun! I'll call you if the place burns down."

I responded, "Don't call me. I won't know what to do. Call the fire department."

And from that day forward, when I wasn't at work, the cell phone stayed on silent.

I am certain this mindset is what has catapulted my success in business. I have created a half dozen businesses that focus on creating a new path. Opening new doors. Creating new industries, all with like-minded individuals. Individuals who were empowered to make decisions. Individuals who were invested in our collective success. Individuals who made it easier for me to leverage my time so I could spend my day growing my life instead of "putting out fires."

ACCOUNTABILITY

We are all accountable for our actions; their affect and influence on our lives and the lives of others.

Sameh Elsayed

Over the years, I've come to realize that people who are comfortable and confident in their own skin are the first to recognize their shortcomings, while people who are insecure and self-conscious are quick to pass the buck. One of my favorite things about being a leader, about being the CEO, and about being an entrepreneur is requiring, recognizing, and rewarding accountability.

True leaders are certain of their skills and take ownership of what happens as a result of their actions.

The simple truth is that most people, including business owners, employees, family members, and, of course, the kids raised by them, *don't* take responsibility for their actions. Without accountability in place, individuals blame others for their actions and find ways to justify their behavior. The best thing about creating a culture of accountability, from the top to the bottom, is that everyone understands the expectations.

I believe "I'm sorry" are the two most powerful words in the English language. For many business owners and managers, these two words are very difficult. I have worked with and for business owners who would sooner chop off a limb than apologize to a subordinate. Do they see apologizing as a sign of weakness? For me, it's the complete opposite. If I can quickly resolve a conflict with an honest, heartfelt apology, then I am happy to do so. I don't always get it right, and my team doesn't always get it right, and taking ownership and applying a quick resolution is, in my mind, the truest form of accountability. The next time you're faced with a conflict, try the apology route. It's incredibly powerful, and it's cheap.

How about You?

Do you hold yourself and others accountable? Do you believe aiming high means having the courage to think outside the box? Do you ever consider training in a whole different avenue or choosing a path that hasn't even been discovered yet?

During my early entrepreneurial days, I sometimes held jobs outside my businesses when they aligned with my calendar and schedule. I was asked to teach at a local university, I judged auditions, and I was a consultant for a small business start-up. I loved getting outside my comfort zone, expanding into new territories, and testing the waters in unknown positions. I also loved these outside experiences because I was constantly growing as a leader and keenly aware of how I was treated when I was an employee versus an owner. All of it helped me aim higher and showed me where I could take even more accountability and inspire it in my employees and students.

As an educator, the opportunity to train dancers at the university level helped me solidify my position and my stance on remaining accountable to all my students, their families, and the community. As the college and university programs became more and more competitive and acceptance rates dwindled, I became acutely aware of the responsibility we have as educators to help our students realize their passions, their dreams, and their potential. To help them facilitate their dreams, wherever those dreams take them.

In early 2021, I got a call to host a *World of Dance* audition series. I was humbled and honored by the invitation. Hosting a *World of Dance* audition series event was a dream opportunity and a great way to showcase the talent in the New England dance community. With the global name recognition alone, I knew it would help aspiring dancers achieve their dreams. As a participating organizer, I would have a key role in ensuring that the event ran smoothly and that all the participants would have a positive experience. Again proving that if you aim high, if you remain accountable to your mission and vision, doors will open.

In case you're wondering, although the *World of Dance* affiliation was an amazing opportunity, I haven't gotten to meet Jennifer Lopez—well, not at the time of writing this book, but give me time!

So why not eliminate the limits? The obstacles are different for all of us. It's not where we are today that counts but where we aim for tomorrow. So why not aim higher? As an entrepreneur, you may have the fire deep down in your belly that can't be extinguished, or you may have a client, employee, or student who has that fire, so why not help everyone aim for more?

And to make good on those aims, you must be accountable. Why be accountable? Because everyone is watching. And if you have trouble with accountability, it is most likely an issue of confidence and cementing your convictions. Good news: Confidence can be developed. Confidence can be strengthened. Confidence can be learned. And once you have confidence, you will stand strong in your convictions.

Like any skill, confidence has to be nurtured and developed. Confrontational and confident are very different and yet sometimes confused for the same thing. I see confidence as how you view yourself when no one is watching. Do you trust yourself? Have you earned credibility with yourself? It's hard to earn credibility with others if you haven't earned it with yourself first.

So start with small things to lay the foundation. If there's conflict, try to see the opposite perspective without becoming defensive. Recognize the "right" answer even when the "right" answer isn't yours. The best part of leading with confidence, and then conviction, is that you will be okay when people disagree with you. You won't see a different point of view as an attack on your beliefs. When you are steadfast in your convictions, it doesn't matter what the opposition says. We can agree to disagree and still be friends. You can't wait to build confidence until after you're successful. You build confidence in small, incremental steps, so you can solidify your convictions, which leads to your success. And the more unwavering you are in your convictions, the more extraordinary your success will be.

If you take credit for the successes in your life, you must also take credit for the failures. If you believe people when they tell you that you're great, then you must believe them when they tell you that you are not. This is what accountability looks like. With experience, I learned to see feedback not as daunting or threatening but as an opportunity to aim higher. Every interaction is an opportunity to grow, an opportunity to build a bridge, or an opportunity to build a bond. If you give the negative feedback just as much weight as the positive feedback, you will elevate your status as a leader.

That is the key—the key to your *aim* and *accountability* in a wealth-oiled machine.

Set your goals and your vision high with no apologies. Don't just let your dreams rest on a piece of paper or a sticky note—let them be tattooed on your forehead for all to see.

If you think "differently," then embrace it. If you are focused on creating something new, doing something unique, then don't let anyone stand in your way. If you choose to follow the path that others have laid out, then make that path a bit steeper. If you choose to carve a new path, have faith that although the road is bumpy and sometimes treacherous today, that same path will someday be the path for others to follow.

Create a culture from the inside out that exudes trust and transparency. Learn from your shortcomings and take corrective action to prevent repeated inconsistencies. When the people in your circle are empowered to make mistakes, you will see how quickly those mistakes diminish.

NOTES

CHAPTER 4
Love and Loyalty

Ready for Change

"I need a personal day next week. My son has a soccer game," said one of my employees who had been with me for almost ten years. She didn't have to ask my permission. She had unlimited time off. Paid sick days, holidays, vacation days—she had earned them.

"Of course," I said. "Of course" is what I always said.

She ended up taking off maybe two hours in total before she came running back in time for her last three classes.

"You didn't have to come running back," I said.

"But I wanted to. I hate to miss work," she replied.

She didn't have to come back because she got paid for the full day whether she was there or not, and yet she still chose to come running back.

We chatted later that night, and she again thanked me for the flexibility. I reminded her that the business was founded on the highly skilled high performers who made up the DNA of the company. My primary job as CEO was to make it easy for the people around me to be successful.

As a young teacher and business leader, I knew exactly how I wanted to be treated. So in turn, I knew exactly how I wanted to treat others.

The truth is, in my businesses, or any business, sometimes work comes first. Sometimes we miss that soccer game. Sometimes we make sacrifices, and sometimes we don't have choices. So it was imperative for the people who supported my business and my business culture to understand: *I set the bar high and expect excellence, so if you can achieve that, if you can continue to exceed my expectations and still make it to the soccer game, then you never have to ask my permission.*

Making it easy for the people in my company to thrive was non-negotiable. I surrounded myself with people who inspired me, who challenged me, who supported me. They believed in my vision and they supported my mission. And because of that, it was important for me to make it easy for them to stay. Make it easy for them to not work *for* me, but to work *with* me. Make it easy for them to love their job.

Love and Poaching

As a teenager, it was challenging for me to reconcile all the amazing parts of the dance studio culture with all the difficult ones.

There was a sense of team and comradery that was hard to match anywhere else. I loved that part of the dance studio community. I loved the team's commitment and accountability to each other. I loved wearing my team colors and representing my studio with confidence and pride. I loved the work ethic and dedication that was expected at every level.

Of course, there was always some jealousy and cattiness that went hand in hand with a bunch of young teens being thrown together into small spaces. Everyone expected to compete for spots, hierarchy, and praise. But I'm all for healthy competition. I loved the relationships that were formed in the dance studio, even when they presented challenges.

I also loved my mentors and teachers, and I think that's why I struggled so much with the hypocrisy when the dance model got it wrong. One minute, a happy family, the next minute, someone was being ostracized with no peaceful resolution. Sometimes, if a parent made a complaint or a student missed an important rehearsal, the expectation was to unite against the "deserter." It was something that didn't align with the lessons preached by most of the studios of my generation: loyalty and commitment.

That was always the struggle for many dancers, employees, and business owners—navigating the minefield. There's a reason people associate dance with drama and dance moms. Unfortunately, the reputation had merit, but it didn't have to be the narrative.

The dance studio industry had a business model that believed the "art" was more important than the systems. A model that celebrated passion but not always purpose or paychecks. A model that believed everyone should be loyal, no matter the circumstances, no matter the relationship. A model that replaced personal connections with emotional inconsistencies.

I was a junior in college when I started putting my business plan together. In addition to teaching at the local dance studio, I was also working mornings at a local day care center. I had a full college course load and I was a dance major, so I had a rigorous dance rehearsal schedule. I worked nights as a telephone operator and weekends as a waitress. I barely had enough time during the day to use the restroom, never mind put up with drama. I was saving every penny for my grand opening just shy of one year away, so I took odd jobs and worked around the clock to make ends meet. The dance teaching position was the only job that really didn't fit well into my schedule. But it was my passion to work with the kids, and it was on-the-job training for my future, so I had to figure it out.

Throughout this time, I was constantly comparing the four jobs I held. What made them unique? Was it the cultures? The leadership? They were all so different, yet their core values on paper were identical: Loyal to Our Customers, Family Atmosphere, Love for What We Do. The jobs were all service industry specific on paper, but they were so different in reality, each with a different set of standards. From the outside, the brand identities told one story, but the culture from the inside—that was the true storyteller.

In the dance studio where I taught on Saturday afternoons, the pay was minimal, and the environment was challenging for many reasons. Teachers were regularly underpaid and overworked, and if parents questioned the policies, they quickly found themselves on the outside looking in.

I started to ask questions. Lots of questions. I asked dancers, parents, and the other teachers why they stayed. I knew why most teachers stayed—for their students. But why would paying customers stay in an environment where drama and conflict seemed unavoidable? Was it because each studio's culture was the same? Was it fear? Was it the product? The answers surprised me.

They stayed out of a sense of "loyalty."

They had the swag and the bumper stickers. They had drunk the proverbial Kool-Aid. Just like a favorite sports organization, they were a team. They were committed and all united by this one thing they all shared—their love for dance and their loyalty to the organization that got them started.

My heart broke as I watched this loyalty play out in the life of one young dance teacher. She had taken on a new role as a faculty member at the dance studio she grew up in and was trying to navigate the expectations of the position. She had just graduated high school and was struggling with the time commitment and the rigorous schedule. As a young dancer, she had forsaken all other activities for her dance studio commitments, even missing her junior prom because it conflicted with a studio event. She was loyal and obedient. She never made waves. She was the picture-perfect student. But now, as a young adult, her schedule and interests were changing, and she didn't want to disappoint anyone, especially not her former teacher and mentor. She feared that voicing her needs, concerns, or opinion would result in ostracism. She grew up completely aware that the dance industry model wasn't a democracy. You did what you were told. You followed the rules.

She had obligated herself to a position that didn't serve her, and yet she stayed. She wanted to be loyal. She wanted to be dedicated. She wanted to remain a part of the community she loved.

I reminded her that loyalty only works in a relationship if it's reciprocated. That sometimes the dance industry was unfair and made assumptions about commitment levels that weren't based on facts. That service wasn't servitude. That she was the only one with the power to change her circumstances.

I reminded her, most importantly, that we teach people how to treat us.

The L's in Your Wealth-Oiled Machine: Love and Loyalty

When the customer comes first, the customer will last.

Robert Half

Imagine for a minute that you're heading out to your favorite restaurant. You're meeting friends for your standing Friday night dinner reservation. In the parking lot, you're greeted by the owner of the restaurant, whom you know very well because you and your family and friends have been loyal customers at his establishment for many years. While the two of you are catching up, the owner mentions that he has learned that you skipped last week's dinner reservation to attend the grand opening of the new restaurant down the street. When you confirm, he abruptly stops you at the door and informs you that you are no longer welcome. He strips you of your reservation, leaving you speechless and alone in the parking lot.

Now, I also want you to imagine that earlier that same day, while ordering your morning coffee at the neighborhood Starbucks, someone you know very well walked in behind you. They had a Dunkin' Donuts coffee cup in their hand, so the manager refused to serve them. They were shunned and asked not to return. None of the employees said a word, and everyone in line quietly ignored the situation, including you. You justified your reaction. "This is the closest coffee shop to my house—the best coffee for miles. I can't go anywhere else. I'm loyal to Starbucks." So you turned your head in fear of looking sympathetic to the brand traitor.

These examples may seem exaggerated, almost comical, but in the 1980s, this was tolerated in the dance studio industry. You were either all in, or you were out.

The dance studios that struggled to retain customers and great employees failed to evolve and didn't question the model. The drama and the conflicts just became the nature of the beast. Business as usual in the life of a dance studio. It was an oxymoron for a business in an industry helping to raise our children.

If you're familiar with the hit reality show *Dance Moms*, I probably don't have to explain much further. I witnessed families shunned and isolated for "fraternizing with the competition." There were contracts and handbooks and rules that made simple transactions difficult. It was considered treason to even suggest supplementing a teaching schedule. I saw dancers subjected to unrealistic schedules and then shunned when they left.

For some, it was a totalitarian regime. Choosing cult over culture. You either complied or you risked alienation.

But why? Why was the dance studio business model so different from other service-based businesses? Why was turnover high and customer and employee retention low? What kept some customers loyal despite the level of service? And most importantly, was there a way to fix it?

LOVE

Don't do it for applause. Do it because it ignites a fire inside you.

Hiral Nagda

I started my first business because I loved the work. Because I loved the craft. And the more I developed relationships around the work, the more I fell in love. I am grateful that I never lost sight of my passion and purpose as I grew the business. It's ironic in retrospect, but the simple truth is that the more I shared the love, the more the business grew. The more I spread the love, the more the business grew. The more I served the love, the more the business grew.

Just like a relationship that endures and thrives, your love, your craft, your passion, your business can also weather the tests of time.

My true heart's desire was to create a life I loved living. A life built on the foundation of trust and stability. A life built on honesty, support, and understanding. A life with shared commitments. If I was committed to building businesses rich in strong relationships, then it certainly stood to reason that building personal relationships built on a strong, unwavering foundation was priority number one.

I'm obsessed with the service industry, and I believe service—great service—should be relationship-driven. Understanding the position of everyone involved. Seeking commonality and resolution that benefits both sides. Jumping out of bed every morning because you love what you do and the people you do it with.

Staying inspired and motivated kept me happy and healthy in my profession.

No matter which side of the coin you find yourself—CEO or employee—if you truly love what you do, then burnout, fatigue, and servitude should never be a factor. And if it is, only you have the power to change it.

By the Way

No one was happier than I was to see the Dance Mom series come to an end. The studio educators who spent their whole careers teaching character, integrity, and respect were again forced to defend the industry. The questions surfaced: Was it possible to train incredible dancers and, more importantly, incredible people without drama and manipulation? Was it possible to maintain a healthy relationship in the studio that respected all sides? The answer was absolutely, and I have spent the last thirty years proving it was possible.

LOYALTY

Yesterday's home runs don't win today's games.

Babe Ruth

Full disclosure, I am not by nature a fan of the word loyalty. I believe we should work for our relationships. I believe we build trust by providing value. I wouldn't want anyone to stay in a relationship with me out of a sense of obligation. I only want people to stay in a relationship with me, personally and professionally, because I have earned it.

So it was easy for me to take loyalty off the table. Build businesses where loyalty wasn't the motive. Build businesses where people were not just expected but encouraged to leave (with a hug) when the value was no longer reciprocal. Build businesses where loyalty was based on value. Value that had to be earned, year in and year out. Value that would later create legacy.

So not just acquiring but also retaining customers became my business model. Not just acquiring but also retaining employees became my business blueprint. Developing a system and a process for creating raving fans. Customers and employees who stayed because of value. Customers and employees who were, in fact, like family—real family—with questions and conflicts and then, most importantly, peaceful resolutions.

For the dance studio, I reinvented the paths for employees. I reinvented the path for dancers. I encouraged everyone to set their own timetable. I made it easy for people to do business with us, and I made it easy for our families to do business with others. Most importantly, I didn't consider that my employees and students worked for me but that I worked for them. I worked *for* them, and they worked *with* me.

Getting to the top would take exceptional programs, but staying and surviving on top—that would take a model of consistent value. That would require a change in the dance studio expectations. If I wanted to create a business that was in the top one percent of the industry and would survive for decades, I needed to push forward, innovate, and expand. I didn't waste time wondering if it was possible. I reached higher. I set out to create new standards. All with the same core mission: Create value that serves both sides. Create a business rich in culture. Create a model led by relationships. Keep the personal in and the emotions out.

Thankfully, a lot has changed in the last thirty years. The businesses that understand the customer experience, that understand the relationship between value and loyalty, are the businesses that survive pandemics and economic downturns. The businesses that work to not just meet but exceed expectations, that put customers and employees first, have paved the way for new and improved business models.

A business model that creates raving fans. Raving fans that build legacy.

If you want loyalty in your life, be consistent and create consistent value. If you want loyal fans, raving fans, it takes planning and listening. Life is a series of events. Building a successful business is about building relationships. I subscribe to authentic marketing, the marketing I grew up on. It's not social media, Facebook, and TikTok videos that build legacy—it's connections.

If you love what you do and you continue to add value to your customers, to your employees, to your partners, to your family members. If you continue to create a community of people who know they can trust you, chances are they will stay.

If you own a service-based business that supports children, I have good news for you. Children are extremely loyal by nature. They seek comfort and familiarity and typically don't like change. The lifetime value may be mammoth, so it only stands to reason that we take our responsibility seriously. The responsibility for their growth and development. The responsibility to help them navigate their future.

The partner, the boss, the leader, the teacher, the friend you were yesterday is in the past. Who are you today? Who will you be tomorrow? Those are the only questions that need answers.

You have the power to change the trajectory of someone's life. With great power comes great responsibility, so use it wisely. The future of the people you serve depends on it.

How about You?

Are you doing what you love?

When you love what you do, when you have a talent, skill, or craft that brings you joy and fulfillment, why not share that with the world? It can be motivating and exhilarating to wake up every day and get to do something you love. Especially when you know that *something* is making a difference in someone's life. When you live a life of passion and purpose, you join a club that, sadly, doesn't have many members. Imagine being one of the lucky few and maybe inspiring others to become part of the club!

When you love what you do, you're more likely to invest more time and effort into improving your skills and knowledge. You will set high standards and stay up to date with the latest developments and innovations. Someone has to be the expert—why not you?

I am so passionate about my purpose here on earth that I decided to write this book. Was it scary? Yes! But oh, so worth it.

I have found that loving what I do will never mean I'm spared from frustrations, setbacks, or challenges, but it does mean I will move heaven and earth to find the motivation and resources to overcome them.

If you lose your passion, if the fire burns out, you can rekindle it and reconnect by becoming more engaged. By showing more appreciation for the gifts you have been given. By focusing on the positives instead of dwelling on the negatives. By reminding yourself why you chose that path in the first place and what brought you the most joy when you were first starting out.

Do the choices you make require commitments? Commitments that require effort? Effort that requires patience and the willingness to work through challenges? Are you committed to building connections based on honesty and trust? Committed to shifting from a loyalty mindset to a value-driven mindset?

How did I make that shift?

I reminded myself that past successes do not guarantee future victories. I recognized that past accomplishments or successes are not always an indicator of future success or happiness. I remained focused on the present moment and future goals rather than resting on past achievements.

We make choices every day about how we treat others, and we make choices every day about how we allow others to treat us. Can you leave the personal in and the emotions out? Do you struggle to keep your emotions in check when making critical business decisions? If the answer is yes, that's okay. It can be learned. It can be nurtured. It can be achieved. You just have to choose to do it.

In times of conflict, I sought commonality and resolution that benefited all sides because I understood that if people left, it was because they no longer saw value. And for all my businesses, I define *value* as *promises kept, results measured and exceeded, time respected, and sacrifices limited.*

I know it's a hard pill to swallow, but as you know by now, I don't sugarcoat the truth, and I'm a tear-the-band-aid-off-quickly kinda gal. Instead of looking side to side for the answers, take a deep dive inside. Inside yourself, inside your business, inside your culture. Maybe your product isn't good enough. Maybe your service isn't good enough. Maybe your attention isn't strong enough. Maybe you haven't nurtured the relationship.

We are not entitled to success. We are not entitled to anyone's business. And we are not entitled to any one relationship. People can't be poached or enticed by the new shiny object if they are continuing to grow and thrive in their current environment, so keep the environment rich. And if they still leave, despite your best efforts, if they no longer see the *value* in the product or service you deliver, at least it won't be because you turned a blind eye or became complacent.

I'm a big believer in love, and the exact same wealth formula that I applied to my businesses has helped me be successful in my marriage.

Even after three decades, it continues to be a work in progress because I never want to get complacent about the *one* relationship I value the most. Although I don't think there are any secrets to a happy marriage, I do apply the same diligent, consistent work ethic, will, and perseverance because I want to keep the environment rich and our relationship growing. If I were to boil it down to one thing, I guess it would be the fact that I choose every day to be happily married. And I believe there is a very big distinction between want and choice. You may want things in your life and you may choose things in your life. Sometimes they align, and sometimes they have a different agenda. So I'm always very clear that I have continued to choose the life I crave. I choose every day to wake up and be grateful for the one person who has continued to support and encourage me, all of me, on this journey. I choose love, I choose to be in love, and for me, that has made all the difference.

That is the key—the key to your *Love* and *Loyalty* in a wealth-oiled machine.

When I realized there was no room for complacency in my personal and professional relationships, that's when I discovered the path to *sustaining success*. When I worked not just to meet expectations but to exceed them every day, that's when true love and loyalty followed me. A loyalty defined by character, and a love defined by choice. A choice to stay because the relationship was earned.

NOTES

CHAPTER 5
TIME AND TROUBLE

Common Sense Is Anything but Common

I was married for about five years before I attempted to make dinner for the first time. It was unusual for me to spend any time doing things outside of my skill set, and designing a menu, grocery shopping, cooking—none of that was in my wheelhouse. Going out for meals or ordering in was far more efficient. Everyone got what they wanted, and there was no mess to clean up. I was very protective of my time and more than happy to delegate as many tasks as possible. Household chores were the first to go. My husband certainly didn't mind, as my attempts at laundry early in our marriage typically rendered everyone's wardrobe pink. I was always racing against the clock, so choosing to do the things in my life that only I could do and delegating the rest was a simple formula for success.

Nonetheless, despite the odds, there I was planning a meal from scratch. It was Valentine's Day, and I was feeling a little romantic, so I decided to give it a try. I went hunting for the cookbooks I'd been given at my wedding shower and was relieved when I found them in the basement. I dusted them off and set out to make a memorable dinner for two.

I settled on Italian, something I thought I could reasonably accomplish. There was just one problem. My husband loves mashed potatoes, and I couldn't find a recipe for them in either of the books.

Now, you have to remember this was way before Google and Pinterest and the world of possibilities on the internet. The only lifeline I had was the landline telephone. So I did what I always did in those days—I called my mother for help.

"Mom, I'm making dinner and I'm looking for a recipe for mashed potatoes."

There was silence on the other end of the line. And then my mother said what I expected her to say, "I'll make them for you and drop them off." She had left the restaurant business, moved practically next door, and was a huge help. She cooked five-course gourmet meals and helped with grocery shopping and housekeeping. She even babysat on demand. It was like I had a personal assistant. She was a lifesaver. But this particular night, I was committed to doing it on my own.

"No, Mom," I said, "Thank you, but I'm going to do it myself. Could you just give me the recipe, please?"

I thought to myself, *I'm a successful serial entrepreneur. I can certainly make mashed potatoes, right?*

More silence, and then, "A recipe for mashed potatoes? Honey, it's just common sense. You boil the potatoes and then mash them. There *is* no recipe."

I hung up the phone, and immediately all sorts of questions started swirling through my mind: What size pot do I use? How much water? Do I use the whole five-pound bag of potatoes? Do I wash the potatoes first? What do I wash them with—soap? Peel the potatoes? Cut the potatoes? If I cut the potatoes, what size should they be? How long do they have to boil? How do I know when they're done? Do they cook for five minutes or an hour? And the most important question of all, do I strain the potatoes before I mash them or mash them in the water?

Turns out I got a few things wrong.

Instead of making mashed potatoes that night, I made five pounds of glue.

Time and money wasted. But I did solidify my position on two fundamental principles:

One, everyone should stick to what they're good at. And two, common sense is anything but common.

Before I called it systems and procedures, I called it recipes. The mashed potato fiasco during Valentine's dinner taught me the importance of having step-by-step directions for success in all aspects of my life, especially in business.

So I created a business "recipe" book. The book sat on a shelf in my office for years. Every time I completed a task, I wrote down the recipe. It started out very simple. This is how we do… What do I need? Who does it serve? How long should it take? What are the ingredients? What is the preparation? What are the step-by-step instructions? What should it look like when it's done?

Each recipe was one page with the exact, concise, step-by-step procedure articulated so anyone could pick up the recipe book at any time and be successful. This book became incredibly powerful because it became my business bible—my business playbook. It was our road map for success. It made my business more efficient and predictable, which made it more profitable. Having this recipe book in place allowed me to provide structure and consistency in the operations. Having clear and concise systems in place helped ensure that high standards could be met and repeated. I was determined to deliver high-quality results, so I needed easily repeatable, high-quality systems. I was obsessed with building trust and a reputation for excellence, so everyone across the board had to be accountable for the outcomes. The only way to make people accountable was to make the systems easy to follow, easy to understand, and easy to repeat.

Well-defined systems and procedures helped me streamline the processes and reduce errors. I was able to support my employees because they had a clear road map. We all worked more efficiently, which saved time and money. When anyone new joined our organization, it became easy to show them and say, "This is how we do things here." This approach helped new employees become effective team members faster.

Continuous improvement became our goal. By documenting consistent systems and procedures, I could predict outcomes, track performance, and identify trouble. I could make adjustments because the foundation was laid. I put the right people in the right places. People got to work on the recipes that were in their skill set. I kept the recipes that brought me joy and delegated the rest. Because trial and error were minimized and the results could be measured and consistently repeated, the business became a well-oiled machine, just like any successful franchise organization.

Goodbye, Multitasker

I was a master "juggler" in high school. I had a ton of extracurricular activities. I had an active social life, a part-time job, a steady boyfriend, and I was committed to one event or another every weekend. But as I got older, I had to start making the tough choices.

I was in the middle of a dance rehearsal when the school chorus director showed up unexpectedly at my dance studio. She had come looking for me because she needed my help choreographing for an upcoming competition, and at the exact same time, my cheer team was at a playoff football game without me. And the theater director had called me at home that morning to remind me of a rescheduled dress rehearsal that had been canceled due to snow. And it was my boyfriend's eighteenth birthday, so I had surprised him with tickets to a comedy show. Everything was scheduled for the same day, practically at the same time. My days of multitasking were over.

That's when I started paying attention to my priorities, my skills, and my interests, and I became completely devoted and committed to the job at hand—no multitasking, no juggling. Completely finishing one objective at a time, one activity at a time, one project at a time. I was 100 percent in until it was time to move on to the next thing. My attention was no longer divided, no longer strained. When I made time for personal relationships, I was present. I wasn't racing against the clock to fit everything and everyone in. I concentrated all my efforts on being successful in that moment, regardless of distractions.

Before this, I always considered multitasking a superpower—a valuable skill set—and I prided myself on the fact that I could do many things at once. But the truth was, I couldn't do many things at once... *well.*

Letting go of the idea of multitasking was challenging at first, but with practice and intention, it became quite easy. I just had to prioritize tasks, prioritize my schedule, prioritize my day, prioritize my time. I focused on just one thing—the one thing that called to me. I honored my schedule and protected myself in my day-to-day routine, which became a game-changer for efficiency. What started out as a challenge became a way of life. A way that led to better grades, better health, better relationships. A way that led to less stress and more productivity in my personal and professional endeavors.

The truth is that I chose to become an entrepreneur because I wanted to leverage my time. I wanted complete control of my calendar. I wanted the biggest return on my investment, and my investment was the *time* I spent developing skills to help me build businesses and enhance relationships that mattered to me.

The T's in Your Wealth-Oiled Machine: Time and Trouble

There is one kind of robber whom the law does not strike at, and who steals what is most precious to men: time.

Napoleon Bonaparte

Balance on One Foot

I remember listening to a bunch of different business/life coaches right after I got married and started my business. Their talks about time management and the balance between work and family were inspirational. I bought all the tapes and listened to the cassettes in the car as I drove to and from work. I wanted their guidance. I wanted a routine for success. Having success as an entrepreneur, wife, and mom were all equally important to me—as important as breathing. If one didn't work, then nothing would work.

There was one particular life coach who I listened to faithfully until I heard that he was getting divorced. I never listened to him again. In retrospect, I realize that may seem immature, but truthfully, I felt so disappointed—almost betrayed. My parents' marriage had ended after twenty-five years, and I was desperate to find answers, desperate to find the "secret." The secret to success both personally and professionally. Was it possible to sustain a healthy relationship? I certainly understood that there were many reasons why marriages didn't work and businesses failed. I also certainly understood that there were times when a relationship needed to end. But from my perspective, there was no gray area. I wanted it to last. And, most importantly, I wanted it to outlast.

But it seemed like everyone was sacrificing. Was it possible to live a balanced life? Was it possible to beat the clock and have the "best of both worlds?" Was it possible to build a successful personal and professional life? And if I only had twenty-four hours in a day, the same twenty-four hours everyone else had, how could I leverage that time so it always worked for me and not against me?

It had worked for me in school, but now the stakes were higher. Would I be able to do it all? Would I be able to live two lives in one body?

I knew entrepreneurs who were experiencing burnout. I had business friends who were fighting the fatigue associated with balancing work and family. Trying to find that extra hour in a day. I had colleagues who were fighting the demands of the calendar and the time restraints on their daily lives that ultimately robbed them of their freedom. I heard a lot about the toll their business was taking on them and little about the joy they had once experienced.

I had joy—tons of joy. I was intentional with my time and my day. Was it possible to sustain it? Was it possible to equally prioritize the demands of a career with the demands of a personal life? Was it possible to continue to add value to all of the relationships in my life that I loved?

I set out on a mission to prove it was possible. Prove that I could be a successful CEO and a happy housewife. Prove I could be the boss lady and a stay-at-home mom. If it was possible to live a life of riches both personally and professionally, then I was determined to find it. I looked for the people who were doing it, living it, excelling at it, and then I followed them.

TIME

Ordinary people merely think how they shall "spend" their time; a man of talent tries to "use" it.

Arthur Schopenhauer

All those coaches talking about time management kept using the term "balance." I understood balance. I taught balance. And what they were saying didn't exactly resonate with what I knew about balance as a dancer or a woman managing a career and a family.

Most people describe balance as the *even distribution* of weight. But in my view, balance is not about keeping things equal, it's about shifting your weight to where it is needed and then moving forward.

If you stand up and put your weight equally on both feet, you will quickly learn that it's impossible to move forward without shifting all your weight to one side.

I wanted to move forward in my life, so I intentionally and deliberately shifted the weight to where I was needed.

When I was at work, I was 100 percent at work, moving that part of my life forward. When I was at home, I was 100 percent at home, moving that part of my life forward. Wherever I was, I was always being supported by the other side. I was never overscheduled. I paid close attention to my time. I didn't keep a color-coded calendar. In fact, I let the day dictate my schedule. Every Monday, I… Every Tuesday, I… And so on. Ten minutes after opening my eyes in the morning, I hit the ground running—no scrolling, no procrastinating.

I chose to do the things in my life only I could do. The rest could go to someone else, and so it did. (Except in the case of that one Valentine's Day dinner, and we saw how that turned out!)

We have all heard the story of the absent-minded professor. We probably all have a "professor" in our life. But I don't believe the absent-minded professor is absent-minded at all. In his skill set, he's a genius; but outside of his skill set, he just isn't. I think it's that simple.

If I came to work for you in your business, and you put me where I have a high skill set, you would rave about me to everyone you know: "This new employee I just hired, she is amazing—a real game-changer." But if you put me outside my skill set and you don't give me a clear routine for success, you would rant about me: "This new employee I just hired, she's an idiot—no common sense."

There is a very thin line between rave and rant.

Because time is our most valued asset, doesn't it make sense to focus on what we do best and provide those around us with a recipe for success that starts with putting them in a position where their talents can shine? In a world of alarm clocks, calendars, and schedules, isn't it less stressful to know you have the right people, in the right places, doing the things that have led to their track record of success? That you have established a routine for those people so they know exactly what to do every single time to achieve the best results?

So if I was committed to only doing the things in my life that only I could do and delegating the rest, what was the struggle?

It came to me one cold morning right before the holidays when I was on my way to work. I was again listening to one of the gurus preach about work-life balance when I stopped the cassette tape. It hit me like a bolt of lightning. It wasn't the work-life balance I was missing. It wasn't a balanced life I was seeking. What I craved was *harmony*.

So I experimented with the different chords in my life, creating progressions and melodies. I paid attention to the different relationships between the notes, the intervals, and how they created tension and resolution. I considered the form of my life and how each piece and element contributed to the overall sound and silence. Two-part harmony, three-part harmony, four-part harmony—the combinations were endless. My life became my symphony, and I played it full out—always aiming for clarity and perfect pitch while always staying true to the one composer—me. Using all the instruments that I loved in my life—the instruments that God gave me to play to my heart's content. Playing all the instruments to their fullest potential, I created the life that I wanted to live—my life, and nobody else's.

The distinction here for me was that I became an entrepreneur to create options. Sometimes those options took me to work and I missed family experiences. I loved to work, but when the trade-off was no longer serving me, I made adjustments. The point is that I don't believe in the theory that we should strive for work-life balance. The pressure to achieve work-life balance is, in my opinion, unfair and unattainable. How do you balance things that, at any given time, aren't measurable in weight? Sometimes for me the work weighed more. Sometimes my family weighed more. Sometimes my husband weighed more, or one child weighed more. I was never concerned with balance but with harmony. How do the pieces of my life fit together when they may never be considered even? How could the varied notes of my life work together like a symphony to support each other? How do I reconcile the give and take on my terms… for my life? How can I manage being a stay-at-home mom during the day and a business mogul at night? The answer for me was *harmony.*

TROUBLE

The trouble with most of us is that we would rather
be ruined by praise than saved by criticism.

Norman Vincent Peale

Anyone who knew me knew that I always had a notebook in hand. I created goals and wrote them out daily. The goals were specific, timed right down to the exact month and year, meticulously laying out my life from the age of eighteen to thirty. It was my life plan. My vision quest.

Each goal was clearly labeled: when I would open my first business, when I would get married, when I would have my first child and second child, when I would open my second business, and so on. I didn't consider it a dream because it was real to me. I could see it, smell it, even taste it. Sometimes people would warn me and chime in: "Be careful what you wish for," and "You make plans and God laughs." It's not that I ignored them—I heard what they said. Sometimes their words of warning would haunt me. But despite the taunts, I stayed the course and spent the next twelve years patiently crossing each goal off the list.

I remained consistent even when the negative thoughts crept in. I understood that as an entrepreneur, my need for clarity was tied to my health and happiness. When I lingered or struggled to be clear, it wreaked havoc on all areas of my life. So I stayed committed despite the fear of not knowing enough or not being enough.

The truth was, every time my business grew, we were presented with new challenges. It may have been easier to play it safe. Stay comfortable. But the roads of resilience and persistence were the only roads that led to greatness. I had a plaque that I kept on my desk for years: "Why not take the extraordinary road, especially when the road to mediocrity is far more crowded?"

The initial 800-square-foot studio grew to a 14,000-square-foot complex with seven classrooms and thirty team members. Our other businesses were also scaling and thriving. All in all, we had over one hundred employees, an eight-figure balance sheet, and thousands of happy customers.

I was living a really lovely life. Wonderful husband. Healthy, thriving children. Successful businesses. I was living the dream. What could possibly go wrong?

I crossed the last goal off my list in 1998. My twelve-year vision was no longer two-dimensional on a piece of paper. I was living it. I had created my life's plan, and at thirty, everything was checked off. Time to enjoy it, right?

But something wasn't right. I was having trouble sleeping and I was becoming increasingly fearful. Fearful that I wasn't going to be able to enjoy the things I had worked for. I started to question everything. *Why did I ask for so much? Why did God bless me with so much? No one gets to live the life of their dreams.*

All the haunts from my past became a theme song in my head: *Be careful what you wish for. You make plans and God laughs. You can't tempt fate without eventually being scorched by it.*

Is that what I'd been doing? Had I been tempting fate?

I became obsessed with doomsday thoughts*: Has God just been waiting for this exact moment to crush me? Has he been patiently waiting for just this time? Waiting until I crossed that very last goal off the list?*

I was disgusted with myself for being so cocky. For bragging about picking the month and year my kids would be born. For having the audacity to build businesses and start a family and expecting both to bring me joy and happiness.

People were suffering all around me—amazing people, kind people. *Why should I be spared?* I was surrounded by people who had their crosses to bear through no fault of their own. People who made good choices, who did everything right. I buried young mothers and stood by as people close to me got terrible diagnoses, and I wondered, *Is my life too good to be true—too good to last? When is the bomb going to go off for me?*

The thoughts started to manifest themselves physically. Soon I had heart pain and numbness. I stopped sleeping altogether, and eating was negligible. Convinced my biggest fears were being realized, I made two or three trips to the emergency room every week. I had gone from never going to the doctor's office to practically living there. You name the test, I had it. I convinced my primary care doctor I was dying, and with each new symptom, he ordered a new test.

You would think the fact that each test came back negative would have cured my hysteria, but I was in the full throws of hypochondria. The more tests that came back negative, the more determined I was to find out what was wrong with me.

My husband held my hand and supported me through my anxiety, but even his comfort and strength couldn't snap me out of it. I was a nervous wreck with my kids. I didn't want them to leave my sight. I spent most nights sitting at the end of their beds, watching them sleep, convinced my time with them was limited.

At the end of a series of CAT scans, MRIs, and ultrasounds, my primary care doctor told me we would be taking a break from tests. He prescribed some antianxiety medication and told me to get some sleep. He also asked me not to schedule any more appointments for one year.

I thought he was crazy. I left his office and within one hour, I had hired a new primary care doctor. A private physician. Finally, I would get some answers.

I paid the thirty-five-hundred-dollar retainer and waited impatiently for the first appointment.

In the meantime, I started asking everyone I knew for medical advice. Complete strangers at my kids' school were consulting with me about my symptoms. I was pulling employees into the bathroom at work to look at bumps on my body. I even pulled the poor girl at my morning coffee drive-through into my obsession. I was consulting with anyone and everyone who would give me their ear, looking for someone to heal me.

The appointment day finally arrived and my husband drove me. I had a list of all the tests I was hoping to have redone, but the doctor wasn't very interested in any of my symptoms. He just wanted to talk.

He asked me about my marriage, my kids, and my work. He asked me about my passions and my dreams. We talked about the things I had accomplished. And then he asked me something strange: "What's next?"

I sat in silence. I didn't have an answer.

He then leaned in and said something I will never forget. "Someday, there will be something to worry about. Until then, why not make today outstanding? You've been busy and you've worked hard. It's time now for you to go and enjoy the life you have built. Why would God give you all these amazing gifts if he didn't want you to enjoy them?" He paused before delivering the final message. "Everyone deserves a blessed life, so go enjoy your blessings."

He encouraged me to go home, hug my husband and my kids, and make a new list of goals for the next twelve years. And that is exactly what I did.

By the Way

I never saw that doctor again, but it was the best thirty-five hundred dollars I ever spent.

How About You?

Are you a perfectionist or have you considered only doing the things in your life that only you can do and giving away the rest? Do you prioritize the demands of your professional life over the responsibilities of your personal life? Have you found balance or harmony? Or do you believe that entrepreneurship is synonymous with sacrifice or, even worse, servitude?

If you allowed yourself the opportunity to work more efficiently, would you produce higher-quality results? Would you avoid the trap of multitasking? Would you turn your rants into raves and live a life of sustained joy?

I make no excuses for the fact that most of my family's meals were eaten out. My kids even went to the local diner every morning for breakfast. (Yes, even on school days.) I shopped at the local 7-11—anything to avoid going to the grocery store—and having a full-time housekeeper wasn't considered a luxury or a guilty pleasure. It was, and is, a necessity.

Of course, I'm not suggesting this for you if the hairs on the back of your neck are standing up. I'm only suggesting the principle. The principle to make choices and decisions that align with your life—your life and nobody else's.

The principle that gives you permission to let go and not be superhuman. To not be the jack-of-all-trades, but maybe just the master of one. The difficult part, of course, is letting go of the story—the story you tell yourself. The story that makes you the only character in every scene. The story that makes you the only superhero qualified to save the day.

And if it's a question of finances, I challenge you with this:

Start small. Make a list of the things you want and rank them in order of importance. Create a budget that takes into account your income, expenses, and savings goals. And then *stick to it*. If you want to consistently have stress in your life, spend more than you make. It's the quickest path to failure and, I think, the easiest one to avoid.

Find ways to barter and trade services. After all, you're talented. There are many talented people in this world, and we can get even more done when we intentionally share and grow the success.

That is the key—the key to navigating your *Time* and *Trouble* in a wealth-oiled machine. Share the wealth, share the time, and share the troubles.

I think most of the time we're so busy wondering what everyone else is thinking about us that we forget about what *we* think about ourselves.

> Today, I am not who you think I am; I am not who I think I am; I am who I think you think I am.
>
> *Charles Horton Cooley*

If you are amazing in one area, be amazing there and create a culture and support system where everyone can celebrate their expertise, where everyone can thrive, where everyone can recognize their worth. Sharing time with like-minded individuals is far different than sharing time with the "same" individuals. Embrace the differences, embrace the people who challenge you and inspire you. Embrace the people who will push you out of your comfort zone, even when it's scary, even when it's uncomfortable. If time is our most valued asset, then it's never been a better time to share the "wealth." To learn and grow with others who enhance our *time* here on earth and, maybe, if we're lucky, soften the *troubles.*

I wish I better understood the workings of this universe and why bad things happen to good people. Unfortunately, I have more questions than answers. So when the fear creeps in, I become even more protective of my life. I understand that my time here on earth is fleeting, so making the most of it, creating a legacy, doing work that I love, and spending as much time as I possibly can with the people who support me is my path for getting through the difficulties.

Someday there will be something to worry about. Until then, let's make today outstanding!

NOTES

CHAPTER 6

HABITS AND HUMANS

This Is How We Do Things Here

"The stronger the routine, the stronger the culture," I said while showing a prospective new hire around the facility and happily answering her questions. Since I'm a big believer in full transparency, I love it when a prospective employee or prospective customer peppers me with questions. My hope is that at the end of our time together, they will have enough information to answer the most important question: Can I be successful here?

She stayed relatively quiet until we got to the end of the tour, and she noticed some large decals encased on the wall in the waiting area: Excellence, Teamwork, Consistency, Resilience.

"Are those the company's core values?" she asked.

"No. Those," I replied, "are our core *habits*."

We took a seat and I continued to explain. "I know a lot of companies have core values, but I'm not exactly sure how you track values. I know in a personal relationship, people may have shared values, but how do you consistently replicate or measure someone's values as they relate to an organization?"

"What do you mean by measure?" she questioned.

"There is only one thing that separates winners from losers in any organization, any game, any team, any sport. It's not talent. It's not money. It's not even grit and perseverance. It's the score. Whoever has the most points at the end wins. So the sooner I can get my entire team headed in the same direction, the better our chances are of winning."

I explained to her that despite our best efforts, despite our talent, despite our resources, sometimes we still can't control the outcome. So the consistency in our approach, in our preparation, becomes the only thing that can be measured.

"Here, we train to win," I affirmed. "Win in business, win in service, win in value. Here, we train our behaviors so they're consistent and repetitive, just like the skills of our dancers. They are our non-negotiables. Here we don't have company core values. Here we have company core habits."

She leaned forward, obviously interested in this new language and approach, so I continued. "Regardless of who enters my business—employee or customer—the rules are the same. We do the same thing day in and day out with the goal of creating results. The goal is always to create value. All routines and rituals are predicated on our core habits."

More leaning and now nodding.

"We aim for excellence in everything we do. Nothing is done in our company if it doesn't serve the *team*. We repeat, replicate, and systemize what is working to create consistency. We do what we say we're going to do, and when we hit obstacles or challenges, our resolve and resilience are relentless. Rinse and repeat."

"What about individuality and creativity? Is it possible to stay unique and creative if the routines and rituals are always shared?" she probed.

I thought this was a great question. "The human characteristics of my businesses have never been lost as a result of our shared habits. In fact, it's much to the contrary. It is in the routine that human characteristics are heightened. I believe cultivating healthy habits and routines keeps all of us moving forward. It actually creates more room for independence because everyone is empowered with the tools they need to be successful."

She cocked her head to the side, clearly processing this possibility.

"We will always continue to challenge each other," I told her. "We will always continue to ask the tough question: How can we do better? Absolutely, innovation is imperative. But the fundamentals that drive the underlying system—that is what becomes our measuring tape, the step-by-step instructions that give us the routine for success, the routine we follow, the routine that helps us win."

She thanked me for my time and as she headed toward the door, I called her back to ask the one question I asked every prospective employee: "Are you committed to excellence?"

She smiled, answered affirmatively, and has been a valued member of our team ever since.

Healthy Habits

In college, I lived paycheck to paycheck, sometimes burying my head in the sand around finances or blaming my poor math skills. That all changed the day I opened my first business. If I was going to lead by example, if I was going to model success, then I would have to become the CEO of my business. Not a dancer who opened a business, but a business owner who just so happened to dance. I wanted to be of service, but I wasn't willing to be in servitude. I knew that if I was going to have longevity doing something I was passionate about—something this important, something this impactful—then burnout, stress, and overwhelm could not be part of my job description.

Developing healthy habits around time and money management became my top priority. Changing my mindset about money and organizing my day-to-day activities into a step-by-step routine became my path.

I created steps around finances—steps that I was committed to. I paid myself first and put together a yearly budget, a monthly budget, and a weekly budget. It wasn't about that one "wealth" number but about the percentage. My input always exceeded my output. I made sure the businesses were healthy and thriving. I woke up every day, poured myself some coffee, and checked my numbers. Every day, without fail.

I also designed a routine around my health and wellness. A routine I could perform daily. A routine that allowed me to stay energized and enthusiastic. If a decision or habit didn't get me where I wanted to go, I changed it. I made better decisions. Better decisions led to better choices, which became better habits.

These core habits became my theme song: excellence, teamwork, consistency, resilience. Habits that became my measuring tape. Habits that allowed me to be successful year in and year out. Habits that have remained at the forefront of everything I still do today, three decades later.

The excitement of opening that first business sent me down the serial entrepreneur path, and I have since built, coached, and consulted on dozens of businesses, all with a similar mission: Do better. When someone was doing something extraordinary in business, I took note. When someone was doing something extraordinary in their marriage, I took note. When someone was doing something extraordinary with their children, I took note. What were the steps they were taking? What were their everyday habits?

Success leaves clues.

Or I should say, patient, deliberate success leaves clues.

The H's in Your Wealth-Oiled Machine: Habits and Humans

The way we do anything is the way we do everything.
Martha Beck

I believe the best part of being human is our capacity to learn and grow. There is no limitation or expiration date on what we can achieve. So I learned, and then, most importantly, I took action on what I learned. I truly believe our choices lead to our outcomes. If we tell people that they have limits, they will believe in those limitations. But if we tell people they have a world of possibilities, they will grow up to believe anything is possible.

Whether you think you can, or you
think you can't, you're right.
Henry Ford

When my son was five years old, he loved Batman. He got a Batman costume for his fifth birthday and wore it every day—every possible minute. He even slept in it. One morning as he came charging down the stairs, fully dressed in character and ready to save the neighborhood, I asked him, "Would you like to be a superhero and save the world when you get older?" I was wondering if maybe a future policeman or firefighter was being inspired here.

He pondered my question for only a moment. “No. I want to be a professional baseball player. I want to run and play outside. I want to make diving catches and hit home runs. I want a job where I can play with a group of my friends all day. I want to be a professional athlete.”

Fifteen years later, he was drafted by the Washington Nationals in the third round of the 2015 Major League Baseball Draft after an amazing three years at Vanderbilt University, two trips to the College World Series, and one National Championship.

I don’t think at five he was particularly good at baseball. In fact, I remember thinking he was more of a drama kid than an athlete. But his father had been an amazing baseball player and had a stellar college career, and my son wanted to follow in his dad’s footsteps. That was his dream, so his father and I did everything in our power to help facilitate his journey. If he was willing to do all the work, if he was willing to train, if he was willing to sacrifice, if he was willing to persevere, if he was willing to get knocked down and get back up, then the least we could do was hold the door open for him.

There are five years between my two kids, and when my daughter was five years old, I asked her the very same question: “If you could do anything in the whole wide world, what would you like to be when you grow up?” Even at this age, she was a precocious, independent, strong-willed young lady, so I had a feeling she already had her entire life figured out. She was a dancing queen and loved music. She knew every lyric to every song, and her favorite show was *Total Request Live* (TRL) on MTV. Yup, not *Sesame Street* or *Barney*—MTV. (Okay, maybe not such great parenting.)

I thought for sure she was going to tell me she wanted to be famous—maybe a rock star, a professional dancer, or a movie star—but no. She didn't take long to announce it, and she did it so confidently that although I shouldn't have been surprised, it still startled me. "I want to *own* MTV." I always laugh when I remember her saying "own" because both her dad and I were entrepreneurs, and "own" was part of her vocabulary.

Fifteen years later, she was accepted into the Annenberg master's program at USC, California, for media and communications, and her first job out of college was with MTV.

I tell these stories not to imply that they didn't have a tough road—they did. I'm sure there were many times they wanted to throw in the towel. They wouldn't be human otherwise. But we believed in dreaming big. We believed in working hard to achieve outcomes. For the people who don't really know us, we are often labeled a family of overachievers and perfectionists. But nothing could be further from the truth. We are, however, a family of high performers, and we believed, and still believe, that when you have good habits, when you understand how to support other humans, when you continue to push forward despite obstacles, doors will open.

By the Way

Professional athlete, publicist, professional dancer, chemist, school teacher, nurse, doctor, scientist, stay-at-home mom, entrepreneur… I am equally proud of all of them. It was never about where they landed but always about the journey they took to get there.

HABITS

Watch your actions, they become your habits.
Watch your habits, they become your character.

Vince Lombardi

As a self-proclaimed business junky, I describe myself as the tortoise who admires and even envies the hare. I wish I could skip steps to get quickly to the finish line, but my habits keep my impatience in check. You don't have to leap off tall buildings to get where you want to go as long as you keep putting one foot in front of the other. I am not a gambler. I take calculated risks—risks that are planned. Planned and then executed. Executed and then repeated, again and again.

If you ask any successful business owner, they will tell you, "An uneventful day at the office is a great day! Get your surprises somewhere else." It is the steady, consistent execution of habits that creates an amazing culture and a systemized routine for success. The hare may be more exciting, the hare may be sexier, the hare may be more fun, but it's the tortoise that always wins the race.

Despite being a math flunky, I had developed some pretty savvy business skills. I became obsessed with business best practices. I read everything I could get my hands on, and then I took action. I made smart investments. I paid myself first, and I started to build wealth—real wealth.

I wasn't motivated by money, but what I soon realized was that when you do what you love, the money follows. Building wealth wasn't about buying the Louis Vuitton bags but about knowing that *I could if I wanted to.* Building wealth was about building opportunity. The opportunity to make better decisions. The opportunity to create healthier companies. The opportunity to weather the downturns in the economy. The opportunity to build my family resources and secure my future.

We had systems in place and a formula for excellence. Our processes were being tested and verified. We had created not just amazing businesses, but we were making a difference in the lives of the people we served. We were creating an impact. We were creating a legacy.

HUMANS

It's never too late to be who you were meant to be.

George Eliot

Humans Helping Humans.

Most business books and motivational speakers will always ask you to clarify your *why*, and when you are struggling, the advice is usually to "find (or get back to) your *why*."

But I never concern myself with *why*.

My North Star, my vision quest, my unicorn, has always been predicated on my… *so that.* I made decisions in my life based on my *so that*, never based on where I was (*why*) but always based on where I was going (*so that*).

I married the man of my dreams *so that* I could spend my life with the one human in this world I could walk shoulder to shoulder with. Someone who would challenge, inspire, and support me. Someone who would help me celebrate the highs and soften the lows. A partner who would help me live up to my full potential. Someone who would keep lifting me back onto my feet, no matter how many times I fell, even when the journey seemed insurmountable.

I opened my first business *so that* I could create impact. *So that* I could inspire little humans to see past limitations. *So that* I could use every resource available to me to make a difference in the life of a child.

I have stayed relentlessly focused on improving the service in my businesses *so that* any human who does business with me understands their value. Understands the importance of communication and open dialogue. Understands that my core habits will dictate the outcomes of our interactions.

I worked hard to build wealth in my life *so that* I could change a branch of my family tree. *So that* I could open as many doors for my family as possible. *So that* I could continue to learn and grow. *So that* I could be the best possible wife and mother to the humans who supported me.

I guess lastly, I wrote this book *so that* I could use my history and experiences to shed light on the fact that although everyone's definition of success and happiness is different, although there is no single measure of fortune, there is a general road map that many humans have used to guide them forward on the path.

Whether it is your *why* or your *so that*, my point is—you get to choose. You get to choose what kind of human you want to be.

If you have the power to choose, then why not choose to live with, play with, dance with, and build wealth with human beings who hold you up? Why not spend your time listening and learning and figuring out how to conduct yourselves in such a beautifully human way that the human beings around you want to follow your lead? Why not get really good at communicating, collaborating, and resolving conflict with other humans *so that* peaceful resolution is always the expectation?

However you measure your life, you have the opportunity to choose. Isn't that the best part of being human? What a luxury—to grow and learn with no expiration date. To live a life designed by you and lived by you—a life of abundance. Your life, on your terms. The simple truth is that the humans before you have done it, and the humans after you will do it, so the only thing that stands in the way of you living the life of your dreams is you.

How about You?

Are you the tortoise or the hare? Do you take calculated risks—risks that are planned for—or do you leap off tall buildings, hoping that someone is waiting there to catch you? When was the last time you learned something new? Brand new? Do you succumb to the idea that an old dog can't learn new tricks? Do you let your employees shy away from innovation and new technologies, or are you always looking to learn and grow and evolve?

As a business owner, what do you measure, and how do you keep score? Do you believe that a company can actually prescribe core values? Measure core values? Show me what a company measures, and I will show you what a company cares about.

I measure habits. I measure retention. Retention is my most important number.

Measuring retention is how I measure true wealth in my businesses. It's how I measure impact. I have had an incredible journey and have been blessed to share experiences with generations of humans. Generations of humans that have created a true legacy for me. A legacy I cherish. A legacy I never take for granted.

I created that legacy by sticking to habits, even when they presented challenges, because I believed they were the building blocks that helped me achieve my goals.

Never underestimate the power of routines, systems, and structure. Healthy habits are vital to achieving success. If you can do a minute of something that brings you results, why not do a minute more? Those minutes will become hours, and those hours will become routine, and a routine of healthy, sustained habits can change your life.

Remember to embrace the human connections in your business. Artificial intelligence, automation, and technology are exciting and they may have their place. But I believe the more businesses turn to automation and technology, the more opportunity there will be for the businesses that understand personal connection. The businesses that keep personal relationships and human connections alive will continue to have the advantage, because *humans helping humans* will never go out of style.

Never underestimate the power of empowering all of the people around you. Create programs with access to resources that enable more humans to thrive. Education is a powerful tool, and together we can provide a positive change that empowers everyone around us with the skills, tools, and opportunities to rise.

As a young girl, I had a poster that hung over my bed—a poster that I can still see vividly in my mind's eye almost fifty years later.

> You only live once, but if you live
> it right, once is enough.
>
> *Mae West*

Your "right" may not be anyone else's "right," but the opportunity to live the life of your dreams has always been within your grasp, even when you're stuck and even when you fall. How do I know?

Because I have been there before and I've seen the way out.

NOTES

CONCLUSION

LEAVE A WEALTH-OILED DENT IN THE MATTRESS

My son was the president of his high school class, and on graduation day, one of his classmate's parents came up to me and said, "Some people come into this world and never wrinkle the covers. Your son left a dent in the mattress."

I thought it was such a beautiful sentiment and really honored the contribution he had made to his high school. Although he had only attended that school for four years, he left a legacy. A legacy that lives on today.

As business owners, we can follow the path of least resistance and maybe do just fine. We can create good products. We can have good customer service, good customer and employee retention, and a good business model. Follow along, don't make waves, and never wrinkle the covers.

Or, we can push for more. We can set our sights higher. We can remove boundaries and expect more from ourselves, our employees, and the people we serve. We can leave dents. Dents that change industries. Dents that change people's lives.

How Do You Measure Wealth?

Everyone measures wealth differently. Some measure their finances, some measure their love, some measure their family. For me, I measure the impact. I measure the value. I measure the dents.

We all have the power to create something extraordinary. You don't have to be a genius to win in business or love. You just need to be committed. If it's a wealth-oiled machine you seek, then the system has lived inside you all along. You simply need to train it and refine it.

The **W**ill and **W**ork Ethic to succeed.

The **E**xpectations for **E**quity and excellence.

The **A**im for greatness and the **A**ccountability required to achieve it.

The **L**ove and **L**oyalty to your craft and your people.

The **T**ime to achieve your dreams and the capacity for navigating **T**rouble.

The **H**abits that create consistency and honor **H**umanity.

As you move toward a new level of awareness, you will quickly discover an abundance of *wealth.* A *wealth* of blessings and a *wealth* of gratitude. The experience of living a life on your terms, under your scrutiny, on your timetable.

You have the power to change the trajectory of your life. You have the power to live a life of sustained success. And, most importantly, you have the power to do that for others!

Your wealth-oiled machine can be a reminder that people are born with endless possibilities. They won't remember the trophy and they won't remember the placement, but they will always remember the people in their life who supported them. The people who encouraged them, empowered them, and yes, even pushed them. They will remember the people who didn't carry them over the threshold but who held the door open for them. The people who gave them a hand when they needed a lift out of life's holes. The people who left impressions. The people who left dents.

And most importantly, the people who empowered them to build their own wealthy life by modeling it. A wealthy life led by a strong will and work ethic. A wealthy life that encourages a high aim and high expectations. A wealthy life filled with sustained love and earned loyalty. A wealthy life that protects time and navigates trouble. A wealthy life that is built on a foundation of healthy habits and that understands how to honor humanity even when faced with obstacles.

Your magical life has always been in your grasp, if only you have the courage to stretch for it.

As a dancer, I know a stretch becomes a lunge, and a lunge becomes a split, and a split becomes a leap. So why not just go ahead and take the leap? The worst thing that happens is you fall. But my hope for you is that you build a support system of strong relationships so someone nearby can help you up… and you can leap again.

NOTES

About the Author

Stephanie Kemp is an award-winning choreographer, teacher, mentor, author, and no-nonsense CEO. A self-proclaimed business junky, her obsession with the service industry catapulted her early success from start-up to scale-up, proving service—*great service*—is relationship-driven. She believes it is the responsibility of mentors, coaches, and business owners to help everyone in their organization see past limitations, set high expectations, and earn their worth.

Not a fan of the "everyone gets a trophy generation," she is outspoken and direct about her views on competition and complacency. Her motto, "Do Better," is her personal and professional theme song, which she plays on a continuous loop in her daily life.

A serial entrepreneur, she has used her time-tested techniques, strategies, and lessons to not only sustain her seven- and eight-figure businesses but to endure and thrive for over three decades. By applying her specialized "Wealth" formula, she has built one of the country's largest, most successful dance studios and lives a life of abundance on her terms in alignment with her goals and dreams.

Stephanie is not a mathematician or a scholar and doesn't have an MBA, but she's proof positive that you, too, can build a successful life filled with passion and purpose. Her message to fellow entrepreneurs is "You're not selfish." A life showered with personal and professional achievements is not only possible—it's imperative.

A Special Invitation from Stephanie

If you are serious about shattering the status quo and sustaining your success…

Visit www.StephaniePKemp.com to:

- download questions designed to help you integrate the six timeless lessons in this book into your business and life
- watch our world-class dancers from NEDA Nation and witness the impact of these lessons on young people with big dreams
- learn more about NEDA Nation and the opportunity to franchise and grow your own sustained success with us
- check out my other wealth-oiled machines that are breaking the status quo and sustaining success

ACKNOWLEDGMENTS

This book is the culmination of decades of practical lessons I have learned on the front lines of my businesses and my life.

As you have learned from my story, I have chosen to leave out the low lows and the high highs because my journey is mine. Although I don't share the challenges and obstacles specifically, they have all led to my resolve and resilience and I am thankful for their lessons.

There are far too many individuals to thank, as many have led to my continued learning and development, but I would like to give a shout-out to just a few of them here:

To my entire team for their continued commitment to excellence and sustained success. You are a group of amazing people with whom I LOVE working. Thank you for your will, work ethic, equity, expectations, aim, accountability, love, loyalty, time, trouble, habits, and humanity.

Special thanks to Phil Black, who encouraged *(pushed)* me to write this book in the first place.

A special thank you to Lisa Nichols, whose one line, "If not now, when? If not you, who?" changed the trajectory of my life in 2023.

A special thank you to Amanda Johnson, whose warm cocoon allowed me to sprout wings and fly as a writer and author.

And of course, a special thank you to my family, who continues to support me even when I'm "relentlessly focused" on "what's next."

Made in United States
North Haven, CT
29 June 2023

38356780R00070